D0876258

Experiences of a Special Indian Agent

Experiences of a Special Indian Agent

By E. E. White

WITH AN INTRODUCTION BY
Edward Everett Dale

UNIVERSITY OF OKLAHOMA PRESS
NORMAN

ST. PHILIP'S COLLEGE LIBRARY

Library of Congress Catalog Card Number: 65-24206

New edition copyright 1965 by the University of Oklahoma Press, Publishing Division of the University. Manufactured in the U.S.A. First printing.

ST. PHILIP'S COLLEGE LIBRARY

INTRODUCTION
By Edward Everett Dale

THIS BOOK was first published in 1893 by the "Diploma Press" of the Arkansas Democrat Company at Little Rock. The title page carried the title *Service on the Indian Reservations. Being the Experiences of a Special Indian Agent While Inspecting Agencies and Serving as Agent for Various Tribes; Including Explanations of How the Government Service Is Conducted on the Reservations; Descriptions of Agencies; Anecdotes Illustrating the Habits, Customs, and Peculiarities of the Indians; and Humorous Anecdotes and Stories of Travel*, by E. E. White. The cover carried a still different title: *Inspecting Agencies. etc.* And the spine used *Serving on the Indian Reservations.* Because the first title is obviously too long for present purposes, the book is being reissued under the shorter but accurate descriptive title used as a running head on the recto pages: *Experiences of a Special Indian Agent.*

The original edition must have been very small for few book collectors ever saw or even heard of it. Its author, Eugene Elliot White, was born on a farm near Prescott in what is now Nevada County, Arkansas. His parents, Joseph and Phoebe (Whiteside) White, sent their son to rural school until his education was interrupted by the Civil War, in which his father served as captain in the army of the Confederacy.

During the war and the years immediately following its close, the lad must have read a great deal, and no doubt had some additional schooling for he was undoubtedly a youth of very considerable education when he entered the office of Mr. Hamby, a leading attorney of Prescott, to study law.

In 1875, when only twenty-one years of age, he was admitted to the Arkansas Bar and began the practice of law as a partner of Mr. Hamby. Later, he became a member of the Texas Bar and was admitted to practice law in the United States courts of Indian Territory. On May 6, 1876, he married Mary Katherine Thornton.

In addition to practicing law, he joined his brother in founding the first newspaper in the county—*The Banner*. The name was later changed to *The Picayune*, which was still being published in 1908. While *The Banner* venture proved quite successful, White's effort to maintain a daily newspaper in Hot Springs, Arkansas, failed and brought him a heavy financial loss.

White soon became active in public life. He served Nevada County as district judge for one term, and for two terms in the state legislature. As a legislator, he helped frame the election laws of Arkansas and worked hard to promote the interests of his district and of the state; his ability and pleasing personality won him many close friends.

Among them none was closer than his fellow townsman, Thomas Chipman McRae, who was later to serve in Congress from 1885 to 1903 and as governor of Arkansas for two terms (1921–25). McRae was three years older than White. He was born at Mount Holly, Arkansas, and had graduated from the law school of Washington and Lee University in 1872. After four years' practice of law at Rosston, he removed to Prescott, where he maintained his residence and law office until his death in 1929. He was active in Arkansas politics, and in the election of 1884, which sent Cleveland to the White House, McRae was elected to Congress. This put him in a position to help his friends, and no doubt he was responsible for White's appointment as special Indian agent. This seems certain since White said frankly that he knew almost nothing about Indians or the Indian Service and was twenty years younger than any of the four other men who at the time were special Indian agents.

Notice of Mr. White's appointment was accompanied by an order to report in person at the Indian Office in Washington. Upon presenting himself to the commissioner of Indian affairs, he was informed that the purpose of the order was to enable him to receive a course of instruction by the department before he entered upon his duties in the field. The commissioner did not hesitate to point out that his youth and lack of experience made this necessary.

White himself had been a little doubtful of his ability to meet the requirements of his new job. He knew that a special agent was under the immediate direction and control of the commissioner of Indian affairs. He might be sent anywhere in the United States to investigate Indian problems, and his reports were to be made directly to the commissioner.

To a great degree he was to be a "trouble shooter" who must expect to be sent to any Indian jurisdiction from which there had come to the commissioner reports of difficulties. Once there, it was his duty to investigate all complaints and report his findings and recommendations. He had a large measure of authority, however, to take such action as seemed needed to improve bad conditions.

As a matter of fact, White had no reason to worry about his qualifications or lack of them for the new job.

Although he was only thirty-one years old, his ten years as practicing attorney, plus his experience as editor of a newspaper and in other activities, had made him more mature than most men of that age. Above all his keen mind, pleasing personality, and delightful sense of humor made him remarkably well fitted for any position which involved dealing with people and their problems.

After White had been given enough instruction to prepare him for work in the field, he was given a temporary appointment to the agency of the North Carolina Cherokees. Unofficially he was told this was done in order to test his ability for field work.

Nevertheless, White was delighted to have this assignment. During his brief stay in Washington he had learned much from the briefing that he had received from officials of the Indian Bureau and his own research. He felt, however, that he needed to learn more before being sent to the large Indian agencies of the West.

The Eastern Cherokees consisted of that group which had fled to the mountains to avoid being sent to the West when most of the tribe had been forced to remove to what is now Oklahoma. Their reservation of some 65,000 acres is a very mountainous area on which lived at that time some nine hundred Indians. The agency in 1885 was at a little mountain village called Charleston, just outside the limits of the reservation. The Indians usually lived in log cabins tucked away in small coves or little valleys where they grew corn, and vegetables and raised livestock. They were a quiet, self-supporting people who had never given the Indian Office any serious trouble.

White thoroughly enjoyed his stay among these people. The Indians were never troublesome, although the region was a favorite haunt for white moonshiners, and he had some laughable experiences when suspected by some of them of being a "revenoor." Funny as these experiences were, he was at times in real danger, for internal revenue agents were regarded as bitter enemies by makers of mountain dew whisky.

After two months with the Eastern Cherokees, he received a telegram ordering him to return to Washington. He reached that city on December 15, 1885, and was immediately ordered to proceed to Kansas to investigate the alleged sale of lands by the Black Bob Band of Shawnee Indians.

This presented a highly involved problem. These Indians had been given lands in Kansas near Kansas City just before the Civil War. During that conflict they had fled to the Indian Territory to seek safety among the Cherokees. A small group of grafters had obtained possession of these patents and bought lands from the Indians at only a fraction of their value. Fortunately, the deeds given by the Indians must be approved by the secretary of the interior.

In dealing with the problem, White's legal training and long experience as a lawyer were most helpful. After a thorough investigation which took him to Muskogee, Indian Territory, site of the agency for the Five Civilized Tribes, to Wyandotte and Olathe, Kansas, and to Vinita and the Sac and Fox agency in the Indian Territory, he made his report recommending that these deeds not be approved. The secretary accepted his recommendation, and the Indians were saved over a half a million dollars while the grafters lost all the time and money that they had put into their fraudulent scheme.

At the close of the Black Bob investigation, White was ordered to Fort Reno to expel the intruders known as "Boomers," who for three or four years had been seeking to occupy the "Oklahoma Lands." To reach Fort Reno, he traveled from Muskogee by rail to Henrietta, Texas. From that little town he journeyed northward by stage across the Red River and the reservation of the Kiowa-Comanche Indians to Fort Sill. The following day the trip was resumed in an old, dilapidated buckboard, so called by someone with a genius for words. This took him past Anadarko, the site of the Indian agency, to Fort Reno on the Cheyenne-Arapaho Indian Reservation near the border of the Oklahoma Lands.

Evidently, White's success in dealing with the Black Bob Shawnee affair had impressed the commissioner of Indian affairs. At any rate, when the officer in command at Fort Reno refused to accept Mr. White's plan for dealing with the Oklahoma Boomer problem, the commissioner readily approved White's telegram requesting to be relieved from further service in the matter and ordered him to visit the agency for the Osage Indians.

After inspecting the Osage agency and making his report, White received a telegram on June 12 ordering him to report *forthwith* to the Ouray agency in Utah, where he would find instructions awaiting him. This pleased him very much, for he had long wanted to pay a visit to this Mormon state. He accordingly boarded the train at Arkansas City to go by rail to Green River, Wyoming. From there the journey had to be completed by stage.

If Agent White had known what lay before him, he would have been anything but elated by his new assignment. The Ouray and Uintah reservations lie in what is known as the Uintah Basin, and until a highway was built crossing it, over forty years later, it was one of the most remote areas in the United States. The nearest railroad points are Green River, Wyoming, about 160 miles to the north, from which the mountains are crossed at Diamond Pass, and Price, Utah, approximately one hundred miles to the south. From the latter the road crosses the mountains at Indian Pass. Both of these passes are blocked by snow for six or seven months of the year.

The Indians on the two reservations were Utes, divided into three groups: the Uintahs, White Rivers, and Uncompahgres. It was the White Rivers living on a reservation in Colorado who in September, 1879, had murdered their agent, N. S. Meeker, and seven of his employees and carried away Meeker's wife, daughter, and another woman. In addition, they had ambushed a detachment of two hundred soldiers under the command of Major Thornburgh, killing the Major and nine of his men and wounding about forty. The remainder of the detachment, entrenched among the rocks, kept the Indians at bay for several days until they were rescued by a strong force under the command of General Wesley Merritt.

As a result, the Indians were forced to give up their lands in Colorado and remove to a new reservation set aside for them in the Uintah Basin of Utah. This new reserve lay between the western boundary of Colorado and the eastern line of the large Ute reservation, and was administered by the agency at White Rocks.

Special Agent White thoroughly enjoyed his trip until

he reached the Green River. Here he was met by Inspector Robert S. Gardner, with whom he was acquainted. Gardner told him that there was serious trouble at Ouray. The Indians were furious because they had been fired upon by white ranchmen while hunting on their former reservation. Also, a survey of the western boundary line showed it to be some miles farther west than it had been thought to be. In consequence, lands which the Indians had believed were theirs were in Colorado. This, combined with other real or fancied grievances, including the theft of money by a dishonest former clerk, had brought the Indians to the verge of an outbreak.

Gardner said that the agent had resigned by telegraph and fled on the fastest horse at the agency, leaving the agency clerk, W. A. McKewen, in charge with nine other employees. He added that he had been at Ouray a week before, but stayed only one night, hurrying back to report the situation to the Department of Indian Affairs. Troops were being sent, but McKewen might be attacked any day. It would be White's duty to try to pacify the Indians and to prevent an outbreak until troops could come to his relief.

With all of his illusions of a pleasant stay in Utah dispelled by Inspector Gardner, White started for Ouray as soon as he could get transportation. As a traveling companion he had a young man who was a clerk in the trader's store at Ouray. They suffered from the intense heat the first day, but on the second day ascended the Uintah Mountains to the summit of Diamond Pass, where they spent the night at a summer sheep ranch. Here they were shown ice an inch thick the following morning. On the third day they reached the agency an hour after dark.

Here White received the instructions referred to in the telegraphic order received at Osage. He was informed of the resignation of the agent and was ordered to take charge of the agency, to pacify the Indians if possible, and to keep the department informed of the situation.

He took over the office as acting agent and met the nine employees, including the chief clerk, W. A. Mc-Kewen, who became his assistant in the trying days that followed. Within twenty-four hours news of his coming had been carried by "moccasin telegraph" to all Indians on the reservation and even to the band encamped off the reservation in Colorado. In the afternoon a messenger came from Chief Saponero asking when the new agent was coming to his camp for a council. To this White replied that he would be busy at the office for several days, but would be glad to talk with any Indians who came to the agency to see him.

A few days later, these Indians and the men of the

band camped off the reservation came to the agency for a council. When no interpreter could be found except a young woman, the Indians refused to hold council with a "squaw" doing the interpreting. Fortunately, the young woman knew of James Davis, a white interpreter at Uintah, and so the council was adjourned until his services could be secured.

Two days later White received a telegram ordering him to proceed at once to Uintah and take charge of that agency also. It added that the two agencies were to be consolidated and that all the Indians of both were to be placed under one agent.

Shocked as he was by the added responsibility, White left McKewen in charge and started at once for the Uintah agency at White Rocks. Here, he relieved the agent, who had already been notified from Washington to be ready for him. For good measure he also dismissed the chief clerk, who was clearly as incompetent as the agent.

The agency employees were very uneasy because the White Rivers had not been about the agency for some days although they were encamped at a secluded spot not much over a mile or so away.

White began to suspect that a few white men must be back of the Indians' threatening attitude. His suspicion was confirmed when a small group of wise old Uintah chiefs came to see him. Their leader, known as Big Tom, made a lengthy speech interpreted to him by the agency interpreter. Big Tom said that for a month some bad white men had been telling the Indians that soldiers were coming to make trouble. Only "two sleeps" ago two white men came after dark to the White River camp and told the Indians that the big soldier chief, General Crook, was coming with his soldiers to kill some of the White River and Uncompahgre chiefs, put others in prison, take the rest of the tribe away, and give the reservation to white people.

He said that the two white men had urged the Indians to attack both agencies, drive away the white people, seize all the supplies and movable property, and meet the soldiers at the mountain passes and drive them back. He added that these white men had told the Uncompahgres the same. The Uintahs were peaceful and thought this was bad talk.

In this crisis White revealed his courage and resourcefulness. He told the Uintah chiefs that it was true that soldiers were coming, not to take away their lands, but to stop this bad talk, to seize and put in jail any bad men, either white or Indian, and to make them safe on their reservation and in their homes. He asked them to take a message to the White Rivers' camp informing them that he wanted their Chief Sosawick and his people to meet him at the agency council house at eight o'clock the next morning. He also asked them to send a runner to Saponero's camp of Uncompahgres asking the Chief to meet him in council at Ouray the "day after tomorrow."

With the departure of the Uintah chiefs for the White Rivers' camp, Agent White quickly made preparations for defense. After the Meeker massacre, the Department of Indian Affairs had sent forty Springfield rifles and ten thousand cartridges to the agency for use in an emergency, but they had never been unpacked. He distributed these among the employees and selected a log house that had a stream of water under it as a blockhouse and put provisions, shovels, etc., inside it.

Soon after dark Big Tom and his men returned. They reported that the White Rivers were ready to fight, but had promised to wait and come to the agency the next morning to hear what the new agent had to say.

Two employees stood guard that night, and the next morning the White Rivers came at eight o'clock. All were heavily armed. The chief had two revolvers buckled on the outside of his blanket, and pistols were protruding from almost every man's blanket. Every belt was full of cartridges, and a Winchester rifle was strapped to almost every saddle.

White had placed twenty chairs in the council house in rows facing two that he had put near the rear for himself and Davis, who had agreed to act as interpreter. The Uintah chiefs had also come to the council, and White placed Big Tom of the Uintahs and Chief Sosawick of the White Rivers directly in front of him. Many other White Rivers gathered about the door, and a number of others remained with the horses. The white employees had been instructed not to come near the council house, but to keep close to their weapons and seem to go about their work.

Davis was wearing two revolvers, and White had one on cach side in a holster and two more thrust into his belt in front. When he rapped for order and rose to speak, he knew that his life and the lives of all the whites at both agencies hung in the balance; but if he could speak in a way that would make his hostile audience want to hear more, such a tragedy might be avoided.

He began by saying that some white men living close to the reservation wanted to take it from the Indians by getting them into a fight with Washington. He said that Big Tom and the other Uintahs came unarmed and friendly and seemed to want to listen, but the White Rivers were armed and looked mad and ugly. He told them that Washington had sent him to many tribes and that he had never needed to carry arms; but when he saw the White Rivers ride up armed like a war party, he had armed himself with four pistols, two for each hand, and armed his people.

"If you will listen to me," he continued, " your country will not be taken from you. If you want me to tell you all about it, I will; but the White Rivers look as if they had come to fight, not to listen. If their ears are closed, I will not talk. If they have come to fight, I want them to begin now. Davis and I are ready and so are the white people outside."

This was a colossal bluff. Agent White knew only too well that in a fight against such overwhelming numbers he and all his employees would be killed within a few minutes. Yet, many Indians, including the chief, would die too, so in a desperate situation he gambled and won.

Sosawick rose and started to explain and make excuses, but White asked him to wait until he heard the whole story. With more eloquence perhaps that he had ever used in pleading the cause of a client, he told them all that he had told the Uintah chiefs the previous evening and much more. He assured them that the soldiers were coming only to protect them against bad men, white or Indian, and not to take their lands. He reminded them of Geronimo, the Apache leader, who had fought and had been sent to Florida, where maybe the mosquitoes would "eat him up"

or the alligators catch him. He told them to return home
and bring their women and children back from the mountains and all would be well.

The Indians were deeply moved by his talk, and the
chief rose and said that they had thought these white men
were their friends but now knew that they were not. He
added that they would have told him of this talk but that
the white men had told them not to. Now, they would
come to him and tell him if there was more bad talk; and
they would help him to keep down trouble. He said that
the Uncompahgres were scared and ready to fight and that
Agent White should go quickly to tell them what he had
told the White Rivers. The chief then shook hands with
White, and the council adjourned.

Apparently the danger was over at Uintah, but White
knew that it was not over at Ouray. Henry Jim, a son of
Saponero, the Uncompahgre chief, and three of four other
young Uncompahgres had heard White's talk and said
that they would ride as fast as they could to Ouray to tell
the Indians there what had been said at Uintah and that
the agent was coming to hold council the next morning.

As soon as possible, White followed them in a buggy,
taking Davis with him. Both were well armed, and while
Indians posted on high points as lookouts stopped them a
few times to see who they were, they reached Ouray an

hour after dark. The employees said that they had been expecting an attack all day for the Indians had bought all the war materials the trader had at the store except what he had been able to conceal. Henry Jim said that when he reached Saponero's camp before night, all the women and children were gone. The chiefs and warriors had planned to attack the agency at daylight, but when told that Agent White was coming, they decided to wait and hear what he had to say.

They came early to the council, and White told them what he had told the White Rivers. They were much pleased, and the council, while long and tedious, was friendly and harmonious. Then the chiefs and warriors promised that if what their agent said was true, he would have their co-operation and help instead of hostility.

That afternoon General Crook reached the reservation with four companies of infantry. They encamped about midway between White Rocks and Ouray and established the beginning of Fort Duchesne. The following day four troops of Negro cavalry arrived, and except for some excitement one night when an Indian boy mistook a group of Indians for "buffalo soldiers," as the Indians called Negro troops, the crisis was over.

White remained as agent until the end of December because no one could be found to relieve him. Four men were offered the position, but all refused it because of its isolation and the notorious character of the Indians. In September, White sent in his report from the Uintah agency and McKewen, his from Ouray, where White had put him in charge as subagent.

In December the Indian Office found a man willing to accept the position as agent at Uintah and Ouray. Late in December he arrived, coming by way of Green River, Wyoming, "on top of seven sacks of Christmas mail on the wobbling little mail sled." On January 1, he assumed the duties of agent, and at long last White was relieved of the most difficult and dangerous assignment of his life.

Considerable space has been given to White's stay at this agency because it would be almost impossible for anyone who had never been among the Indians of the Uintah Basin to realize how remote was his situation or the ability he displayed in preventing a bloody massacre.

In late April and early May, 1927, this writer with only one companion visited the Uintah and Ouray agency as members of the Meriam Indian Survey Commission of the Institute for Government Research, now the Brookings Institution. We came from Price, Utah, over Indian Pass. The agency was then at Fort Duchesne, which had been turned over to the Indian Bureau when abandoned by the War Department.

We visited the school at White Rocks and also at Ouray, where we held council with all the three groups of Indians. Even then, forty years after Agent White had been in charge, the White Rivers still retained their hostility toward all white people and were by far the most insulting and disagreeable Indians that we had met among the fifty or more tribes with which we had held council. The Uintahs were a kindly people and the Uncompahgres fairly pleasant, but forty years had not changed the White Rivers in the least.

When relieved by the new agent, White left immediately for Muskogee by way of Price and Salt Lake City. He had become much attached to the employees and many of the Indians during his stay at this agency and said good-bye to them with sincere regret. Upon reaching Muskogee, he was ordered to investigate the sale of lands by some Shawnee Indians, not of Black Bob's band. This took him to the Sac and Fox agency, to Vinita, and to some towns in Kansas.

After some adventures on a hunting trip, he completed his investigation and was sent to the Osage and Kaw agency at Pawhuska. He was placed in charge of this agency on March 9. Even at that time, before the discovery of oil on their lands, the Osages were said to be the richest people in the world. They had a written code of laws and organized government, but still retained many of their old-time manners and customs. White describes some of these in interesting fashion. Whisky peddlers and a few Boomers seeking to cross the reservation and occupy Oklahoma lands gave him some trouble, but the Indians, very little.

On the first of July, Acting Agent White was relieved by a permanent agent. His few months there must have been pleasant coming so closely after Uintah and Ouray, for he devotes three chapters of his book to a vivid description of the Osages and other Indians at nearby reservations. After leaving this agency, he started at once on a tour of inspection that included the Ponca and the Pawnee, and the Otoe and the Tonkawa, which at that time were subagencies of the Ponca. He then inspected the Sac and Fox, Cheyenne-Arapaho, and finally the agency at Anadarko for the Kiowa-Comanche and Wichita-Caddo reservations. This was one of the most important Indian agencies in the United States. The area of the two reservations was almost the same as that of the state of Connecticut, and the number of Indians on them was at that time over four thousand. On the Kiowa-Comanche reservation there were also some Apaches, while on the Washita-Caddo reservation there were a few representatives of three or four more tribes.

Grave charges had been preferred against the agent, and White was ordered to make a careful investigation. It required some six weeks to complete it, but on October 8 he submitted his report. As soon as it reached Washington, the agent was removed and White was ordered to take charge of the agency until a suitable permanent agent could be found.

This was White's last and longest term as acting agent. He took over the agency on October 19, 1887, and remained in charge until September, 1888, a period of eleven months, before he was relieved by W. D. Myers. Apparently this was an instance when White did not mind the slowness of Washington, for he devotes approximately eighty pages to a description of these Indians and his experiences as their agent.

Much space is given to Quanah Parker, noted chief of the Comanches, including a long extract from an article by General George F. Alford on the life of Quanah's mother, Cynthia Ann Parker. Also, there is the romantic story of Quanah's elopment with Yellow Bear's daughter, Weckeah, who became his first and favorite wife, although he eventually married four more. White had this romantic story from Quanah himself, who had become his close friend. In fact, he became a close friend of many Indians on these reservations as well as of many of the employees of the agencies.

While in charge of these Indians, Agent White was upon ground very familiar to this writer, who lived several years only three miles from the Kiowa-Comanche Reservation and knew Quanah Parker quite well. He was almost revered by most of his fellow tribesmen. His big house near the head of West Cache Creek had wide porches and a red roof on which were painted huge white stars. It was a fitting home for the Chief and his five wives and many children. While Weckeah was no doubt his favorite, he was apparently devoted to all of them. Certainly they were all deeply devoted to him. Some years after Quanah's death the writer saw the youngest wife, Too-nacy. Her sleeves were rolled up, for she was making bread, and across her left forearm were tattooed these words, "Quanah died February 12, 1911."

Upon leaving this agency, White proceeded to Ardmore to investigate conflicting claims to a coal mine. He was then sent to make some investigations at the Cheyenne-Arapaho, Ponca, and Quapaw agencies. The first two required some weeks, but after a week at Quapaw he received a telegraphic order to proceed immediately to Genoa, Nebraska, where a large Indian boarding school

ST. PHILIP'S COLLEGE LIBRARY

was located. He took the first train for that town, but, before reaching it, he read in a morning newspaper that he had been appointed Indian inspector by the President. This was a great surprise, for he did not know of any vacancy in the inspectorships.

White reached Genoa on January 25, 1889. Here he found written orders stating that the superintendent of the boarding school had been removed and that he was assigned as special agent to take charge as acting superintendent. He remained in this position until March 12, when he qualified as inspector. He had served as special agent for only about three and one-half years but had traveled more and had more adventures and thrilling experiences than most men of his time had in their entire lives.

Special Agent White's story ends with his appointment as inspector, but he adds an appendix listing the agencies and industrial schools in the United States with the number of employees at each and the salary of all important positions. To this is added other information on the Indian Service.

Everyone who reads this delightful book will no doubt want to know something of the further life work of the author, whose ability, charming personality, and keen sense of humor are revealed in every chapter. For these

ST. PHILIP'S COLLEGE LIBRARY

readers it should be said that he served several years as inspector in the Indian Service.

His wife, who had borne him seven children, died in 1893. Their first child died in infancy and two more died quite young. In 1895, White, while still inspector, established a home in Washington for his four motherless children.

The following year, he was appointed chief of the Division of Indian Affairs in the office of the secretary of the interior. Until 1907 the various functions of the Department of the Interior were allocated to several divisions, each headed by a chief. In this position he was not in contact with Indians but advised the secretary on all matters concerning Indian affairs. This enabled him to remain at home in Washington with his children, which was no doubt his chief reason for accepting the appointment.

White was eager to establish his own law practice again and on September 16, 1899, tendered his resignation to Secretary of the Interior Ethan A. Hitchcock to take effect on February 15, 1900. On that date he left the service of the United States and soon after removed with his son and three daughters to Sulphur, Oklahoma, where he established a home and resumed the practice of law.

He was active in civic affairs, and in 1902 was largely responsible for the passage of the act of Congress creating the Sulphur Springs Reserve, which in 1906 became Platt National Park. He served two terms as mayor of Sulphur, and at the time of his death on August 29, 1908, at the age of fifty-four, was a city official. He was survived by one son and three daughters. The son and one daughter have since died; but at the time this is being written two daughters, Mrs. James E. Chase of Dallas, Texas, and Mrs. Thomas P. Wall of Tulsa, Oklahoma, are still living. They and a granddaughter, Mrs. Eugenia Stivers of Sapulpa, Oklahoma, have contributed much information on the life of White which is gratefully acknowledged.

CONTENTS

ILLUSTRATIONS

EXPERIENCES OF A SPECIAL INDIAN AGENT

INTRODUCTION.

CHAPTER I.

APPOINTED SPECIAL INDIAN AGENT — ORDERED TO WASHINGTON—SWINDLED AND LAUGHED AT—ACQUIRING ''EXPERIENCE''—TO NORTH CAROLINA.

IN the United States Indian service there are five Special Agents, five Inspectors and fifty-eight Agents. The Agents have personal supervision and control, within certain limitations, of all affairs on the various Reservations, and in many cases several separate Reservations, and several different tribes, or remnants of tribes, are under the jurisdiction of one Agency.

The duty of the Special Agents and Inspectors is to visit and inspect the Agencies from time to time, and investigate all complaints concerning the Indians or affairs on the Reservations. Special Agents are also often detailed to serve as Agents for indefinite terms.

The Special Agents are under the immediate direction and control of the Commissioner of Indian Affairs, and the Inspectors are in like manner subordinate to the Secretary of the Interior.

There being no separate circuits, or prescribed time for the inspection of Agencies, each of the Special Agents and Inspectors has a field of duty coextensive with the limits of the United States, and is required to go wherever and whenever he may happen to be ordered.

Notice of my appointment to be a Special Agent was accompanied by an order to report in person at the Indian Office, in Washington. Presenting myself to the Commissioner, I was informed that the purpose of the order was to enable me to receive a course of instruction at the Department before entering upon my duties in the field.

From the first information of my appointment I had been oppressed with a distrust of my ability to meet the requirements of the service. I was shown at the Department, and, as I fancied, not in compliment, but rather in derision, that I was the youngest Special Agent then in the service by twenty years, and in addition to my inexperience in age, I was a stranger both to Indians and the Indian service. In recommending me for appointment my friends had probably urged, in lieu of experience, my ordinary business qualifications, and what they believed to be some natural adaptability to that kind of service.

When I was deemed well enough informed to take the field, notice was unofficially communicated to me

that I would be first sent on a sort of training trip to the
Eastern Band of Cherokees, in North Carolina. This
information could not have been more acceptable to me
if it had been designed as a special favor, because I was
unwilling to be sent to the large Agencies in the West
until I possessed more knowledge of the service than it
was possible to acquire in Washington.

But having accepted the appointment, I was eager to
veteranize myself and acquire that peculiar accomplish-
ment called "experience." My first lesson, however,
which I received even before I got out of Washington,
like many others which followed, was in the highest
degree unsatisfactory. I may say that it conformed
exactly to my idea of "a mean trick," in my then unso-
phisticated state, and, in addition to wounding my pride
most grievously it cost me a dollar, and, so far as I
know, has never profited me anything in return.

It occurred as follows: On the morning of the day
named in my orders for my departure from Washington,
I went to the Department to receive the special instructions which I had been told would be ready for me at
9 o'clock. But being detained beyond that hour, I
found to my dismay, upon returning to the hotel, that
it lacked only a few minutes of train time. I had
ascertained that I should depart from the Baltimore &

Potomac depot, but was ignorant of its location. I supposed it was somewhere toward the outskirts of the city.

The hotel at which I was stopping is situated on Pennsylvania Avenue, less than half way from the Capitol to the White House. Hurrying out on the curbstone, I hailed a cab and inquired of the driver, and with manifest anxiety, I now have no doubt, if he could get me to the Baltimore & Potomac depot in time for the 10:40 train. Glancing hastily at his watch, he said: "May be I can, if you'll jump in quick." Detecting a rascally gleam in his eye as he said that, the thought flashed through my mind that his intention was to secure my fare, with no idea of getting me to the train. For that reason I told him, and with more vehemence, I am now willing to admit, than was necessary, that I would pay him a dollar—double fare—to get me to the depot in time, but not a cent if he failed.

It was a pleasant autumn day, and a group of ten or twelve distinguished looking men—Senators and Members of Congress, I imagined—were standing in front of the hotel. My negotiations with the cabman attracting their attention, they suspended conversation among themselves and looked at me in an amused sort of way, which at the time I did not comprehend.

As I stepped into the cab the driver sprang to his seat, gave his horse a cut with the whip, and we dashed

nearly straight across the street, stopping in front of a
large brick house just a little beyond, and in full view
of the hotel.   Dismounting quickly and jerking the
cab door open, the driver called out:

"Here ye air!"

"'Here ye air' what?" I demanded.

"Baltimore & Potomac depot.   Train goes in ten
minutes," he replied.

As I alighted from the cab and gave up the dollar, I
looked back across the street.   The men in front of the
hotel threw kisses to me, and *seemed* to say, "Call
again!"   *   *   *   *   *   *   *

I proceeded direct to Charleston, North Carolina.
The Cherokee Reservation, known as Qualla Boundary,
lies in Swain and Jackson Counties, in the extreme
southwest corner of the State, near the line of Tennessee
and Georgia.   Charleston is the seat of the Agency,
though not within the Boundary.

This pretty little mountain town occupies a picturesque situation on both banks of the Tuckaseegee River,
a beautiful tributary of the Tennessee.   Here I had my
headquarters during my stay in North Carolina, a period of two months.   From this point I made several
trips to Asheville by rail, and rode over the Indian
Reservation, and the surrounding country generally, on
horseback.

CHAPTER II.

AMONG THE EASTERN BAND OF CHEROKEES — IN A
HURRICANE.

THE lands owned by the Eastern Band of Cherokees are estimated at sixty-five thousand acres—
fifty thousand in a body known as Qualla Boundary, in
Swain and Jackson Counties, and fifteen thousand in
Graham and Cherokee Counties.

According to the Agent's census report, there are
nine hundred full-blood Cherokees still inhabiting these
lands, their ancestors having been permitted to remain
in that country when the main part of the tribe removed
to the Indian Territory, in 1832.

These Indians receive no annuity, or other personal
aid, from the Government. Most of them own small
farms and some live stock, dwell in log houses, wear
civilized dress, and are self-supporting. The Government exercises guardianship over them, and general
supervision of their schools, through their Agent at
Charleston. Their educational facilities consist of two
boarding schools at Yellow Hill, and five day schools in
other settlements.

After one day spent in council with the Indians on Qualla Boundary, I made a trip on horseback to Murphy, in Cherokee County, to meet those in that locality. Fording the Tennessee River above the mouth of the Tuckaseegee, I fell into the Valleytown Road at the mouth of the Nantahalah, and traveled directly up that stream to its source at Red Marble Gap.

Hid away here in these wild and almost impenetrable mountains, seldom seen by man, and altogether unknown among the great rivers of the earth, this little river is indeed one of the physical gems of this continent. Only twenty miles long, flowing in a due north course, and high mountains rising precipitously from the water's edge on both sides, the sun never shines on it except for a few hours at midday. For this reason the Cherokees call it Noonday River—the beautiful name Nantahalah, as they pronounce it, meaning that in their language.

After two days spent with the Indians near Murphy, and one day with a small band residing on Hanging Dog Creek, beyond the Hiawassee River, I set out for Robbinsville, in Graham County. Coming back on the Charleston road as far as Valleytown, I there turned west across Cheoih Mountain.

Soon after I began to ascend the mountain a heavy rain and windstorm came up. A mile or more further on I actually rode into the clouds. They were banked up against the mountain side, and of such density as to be as dark as night, except when illuminated by lightning. The road was a narrow dugway, and ascended in a zigzag course, with an almost vertical wall on one side, and a gorge several hundred feet deep on the other. The ground being wet and slippery, my horse held his footing with great difficulty. Like myself, he felt the presence of danger. Proceeding cautiously a few steps at a time, he would halt and shiver, and then pick his way slowly on a few steps and stop and shudder again. Heavy thunder, which jarred the earth, and blinding flashes of lightning, which enveloped me in flame, were almost continuous. Several times the wind almost twisted me out of the saddle, and seemed about to lift my horse bodily from the earth. The rain was the heaviest I ever saw. It appeared to descend in sheets instead of drops and streams. I did not seem to be in mere rain, but in *water*.

In the course of half an hour I suddenly emerged from the clouds. Halting and turning my horse around in the road, I looked back down the mountain. I had actually ridden *through* the clouds, and into the sunlight above them. All along the side of the mountain, and far out over the valley, lay the great bank of clouds, rolling and tumbling and rearing up in places, like some gigantic thing of life in mortal combat.

The mountain still rose several hundred feet above me.   Riding on to the summit, I halted there and surveyed the scene again.   It was a scene worth beholding.   The sun never shone brighter than it was then shining up there above the clouds.   Down below, the storm was unabated.   And there on the summit I could see that the clouds extended entirely around the mountain.   The thunder was still booming with undiminished fury.   The clouds were still rolling about in the most violent commotion, and lurid with continuous lightning.   Trees were swaying in every direction, and in the awful roar I thought I could distinguish the sounds of falling timber.

In easy sight were several other peaks also above the clouds.   Sitting there calm, serene and majestic, with their rich green laurel and spruce blended with the sear and yellow leaf of the ash and oak, and bathed in the bright sunlight, their colors made more brilliant by reflection from the dark clouds below, they constituted fit settings in the vast field of roaring, upheaving vapor with which they were girdled about, and added much to the grandeur and magnificence of the scene.

The cold wind on the summit soon compelled me to proceed on down through the storm on the opposite side of the mountain.   By the time I had descended that far the hurricane had spent its force.   Some rain was still falling, and it seemed as cold as ice water. From there on down to Robbinsville every rivulet was a torrent. Some of these flowed across the road, and were almost deep enough to swim my horse. Water was rushing down the mountain side in heavy volumes where there were no streams or channels. The road was washed into gullies, and thereby rendered well nigh impassable, and in some places dangerous. I arrived at Robbinsville just at nightfall, thoroughly wet and chilled, and suffering terribly from cold and neuralgia, in consequence of the exposure.

CHAPTER III.

JOHN JAYBIRD, THE "INDIAN RELIC" MAKER—A
DUDE AND A LAWYER.

WHEN I had completed my duties at Robbinsville, I set out on the return trip to Charleston. At the ford on the Tennessee River I fell in with a young Cherokee named John Jaybird, and rode on to Charleston in his company. Mr. Jaybird is known both among the whites and Indians as "the Indian relic maker." His chief employment is carving the images of men and animals in a kind of clay, or soft stone, found in that locality. With no other implement than a pocket knife he can carve an exact image of any animal he has ever seen, or of which he has ever even seen a picture. For these curiosities, or "Indian relics," as he calls them, he finds a profitable sale among the whites.

A few days after my meeting with him, Jaybird made himself the hero of an incident that was the subject of much humorous comment as long as I stayed in the country.   A dude came out from the city to visit Mr. Siler, a prominent young lawyer of Charleston.   He professed to be fond of fishing, and from the first manifested great impatience to embark in that delightful pastime.   He was very loud, and so extremely blustering and energetic that Mr. Siler's village friends stood off and looked on in amazement, and sometimes in great amusement also.   But Mr. Siler was courteous and obliging, and not disposed to be critical.   Nevertheless, it was whispered about among his home friends that at heart he would be glad enough to get the dude off in the woods out of sight.   Anyhow, he said the dude should fish as much as he wished.

Equipped with bait and tackle, they betook themselves to the river.   To the dude's evident astonishment the fish refused to come out on the bank and suffer him to kill them with a club, and he shifted about too much to give them a chance at his hook.   He could always see a better place somewhere else.   He soon began to manifest disappointment in the fish and disgust for the country, and intimated that the people were shamefully deficient in enterprise and style, and in no respect what they should be.

Rambling on down the river—the dude leading and Siler following—they came in sight of Jaybird, who was also fishing.   Sitting motionless on a rock, with his

gaze fixed on the cork on his line, he seemed the coun-
terpart of "the lone fisherman."

"By jove!   Yonder's an Indian," said the dude;
"let's make him get away and let us have that place."

"Oh, no," replied Siler; "that's John Jaybird, one
of the best fellows in the world.   Let's not bother
him."

Mr. Siler and Jaybird were close friends.

"No," said the dude; "that's the most decent place
I've seen, and I intend to have it; I do, by Jove!"

"Oh, no; don't do that," Siler pleaded; "he
wouldn't disturb us.   Besides, if we try to *make* him
go he's liable to get stubborn, and we had better not
have any trouble with him.   Wait and I'll ask him to
let you have the place; may be he'll do it."

" Oh, get out," the dude ejaculated ; " what's
the use of so much politeness with a lazy, sleepy-look-
ing Indian?   Watch me wake him up and make him
trot.   By jove, watch me!"

Swelling himself up to the highest tension, he strode
up to Jaybird, who was still unaware of their approach.
Slapping his hand down on Jaybird's head and snatch-
ing his hat off, he exclaimed:

"Here, you Indian; clear out from here!   By jove,
clear out!"

Jaybird looked up at the intruder, but with a face as barren of expression as the rock upon which he sat. Comprehending the demand, however, he replied:

"Yes; me no clear out.   Me heap like it, this place. Me heap ketch him, fish."

"Get out, I tell you!   By jove, get out!" roared the dude, with visible signs of embarrassment and rage.

"Yes, me no git out.   Me heap like it, this—"

Before Jaybird could finish the sentence the dude slapped him on the side of the head with his open hand. Springing to his feet, Jaybird uttered a whoop and ran into the dude, butting him with his head and shoulders instead of striking him.   The dude's breath escaped from him with a sound not unlike the bleat of a calf, and he fell at full length on his back.   Jaybird went down on top of him, pounding and biting with a force and ferocity that suggested a cross between a pugilist and a wild cat.   The dude tried to call Siler, but Jaybird put his mouth over the dude's and bit his lips almost off.   He bit the dude's nose, eyebrows, cheeks, ears and arms.   He choked him, and beat him from his waist to his head.

When Jaybird thus sprung himself head foremost at the dude, Siler fell over on the ground in a spasm of laughter.   This did not escape Jaybird's notice, and he jumped to a wrong conclusion as to the cause of it.

Siler always said that he had no idea the Indian was hurting the dude half so bad, but that the turn the affair had taken was so absurd and ridiculous he would have been bound to laugh anyhow. His friends believed that he was simply glad to see the dude get a whipping. Possibly both these causes contributed to his hilarity.

But the conviction had fastened itself on Jaybird's mind that this man Siler, whom he had always regarded as a friend, was laughing *because the dude was making him clear out*. So, while the dude was *performing that feat*, Jaybird kept one eye on Siler and silently determined in his own mind what he would do for him when he got through with the dude.

The dude had scarcely raised a hand in resistance since this human catapult struck him, and now he lay there as limp and motionless as a dead man. Siler had laughed until he was almost exhausted, and was leaning against a sapling, still laughing. Suddenly Jaybird uttered another whoop, sprang from the dude and rushed furiously on Siler. Before the hilarious lawyer could recover from his surprise, he was down on his back, rapidly being pounded and chewed into pulp himself.

The dude dragged himself to the root of a tree, carefully placed his single eyeglass, and began, as Siler expressed it, "to hold an inquest on himself, and take an inventory of his bruises and mutilations." Siler called to him for help. He seemed surprised, and could repress his resentment of Siler's conduct no longer. Readjusting his eyeglass, and taking a closer look at Jaybird and Siler, he exclaimed in a tone of mingled revenge and satisfaction:

"Ah, by jove! You're calling for help yourself now, are you? You played the deuce helping me; you did, by jove! I hope he'll beat you to death and scalp you, and if it were not for the law I'd help him do it; I would, by jove!!"

Jaybird relaxed no effort until Siler was as badly whipped as the dude. Then rising and deliberately *spitting on his bait* afresh, he resumed his seat on the rock, and again remarked in the same half-supplicating tone, though with rather an ominous shake of the head:

"Yes; me no git out. Me heap like it, this place. Me heap ketch him, fish."

None of their bones being broken, Siler and the dude were able to get back to Charleston. The whole town gathered in to look at them, and the affair provoked many witty comments. The doctor said he could patch up their wounds well enough for all practical purposes, but he shook his head discouragingly when asked if they would ever be pretty any more.

Mr. Jaybird came out without a scratch, and Siler said the last they saw of him he was sitting on the rock, gazing at the cork on his line, precisely as he was when they found him.

CHAPTER IV.

A NIGHT AMONG MOONSHINERS—GLAD I WAS NOT RE-
LATED TO OLD DAVE—"UPSTAIRS"—AN UNCOMMON
BEDCHAMBER—THE OCCUPANTS OF THE LOWER
BERTH—"MUST NOT LOOK CROSS-EYED"—ORDERED
BACK TO WASHINGTON.

THAT portion of North Carolina was known in the
Revenue Department as one of the worst moonshine districts in the United States.   Being a stranger,
and traveling alone over the country, I was several times
suspected of being a revenue officer.   Under this suspicion my life would have been in peril if I had come
even accidentally on an illicit distillery, or unconsciously
turned from the main highway in the direction of one.

The first intimation I had of being thus suspected
was on a trip by the wagon road from Webster to
Charleston.   The route lay across a range of mountains,
and, as I had been delayed by an accident, nightfall
overtook me long before I reached the summit.   Just
as twilight was setting in I came to an old mountain-
eer's cabin.   The old fellow was out at the roadside

as I drove up.   He seemed to have been apprised of my approach, and I was much puzzled by the cunning, wariness and evident suspicion with which he regarded me.   At first he refused me hospitality for the night, on the plea that he had not a blade of fodder or a grain of corn for my team, or a mouthful of anything for me to eat.   He declared that he was right on the verge of starvation, and that he did not see what was to become of the country; that if times did not take a turn for the better pretty soon the bottom would ''jis natchally'' drop out entirely.

I reminded him that it was several miles to the nearest house on the road in either direction, and told him that unless he could take me in I would have to tie up my team and sleep under the trees.

''You ain't jis natchally *afeared* to go on, air you?'' he asked.

''Yes,'' I replied; ''just *naturally* afraid.   Besides, as the road is difficult and dangerous, and I have never been over it, I don't believe I could find the way in a dark night, as this is going to be, even if I were brave enough to try.''

''You don't, eh?   What do you call your name, if it's a fair question?''

''White.''

"White?   By gravy!   Any kin to old Uncle Davey White, of Soco Gap?"

"I hope not."

"You don't say!   Well, I'll be hanged if you don't jis natchally know him mighty well fur a man that ain't no kin to him."

"Don't know him at all.   Never heard of him before."

"*Didn't!*   Well, you've jis natchally got the old rascal sized up about right, anyhow.   You have, shore fur a fack."

"How do you know I've sized him up at all?"

"Why, didn't you say yourself jis now that you jis natchally hoped you warn't no kin to the old Republican son-of-a-gun?"

"Yes, and I stick to it, but—"

"Bully fur you, Colonel!   Hanged if I wouldn't stick to it too.   I'm jis natchally glad myself that you ain't no kin to the old rapscallion.   And, Colonel, if it's a fair question, I'd jis natchally love to know whur you'er goin'?"

"To Charleston."

"You don't say!   You hain't lived there long, I reckon.   I ain't never seed you there."

"I don't live there at all, and did not say that I did."

"Don't take no offense, Colonel; don't take no offense. I don't mean no harm; none at all. But, gentle*men*, I'd jis natchally love to know whur you do live, if you don't mind tellin'?"

"In Arkansas."

"THE *devil!* In Arkan—Say, Colonel; my name is Beasly—Wm. H. Beasly, Esquire, J. P., jestice of the peace of Panter Creek Precinct. By grab, I'm jis natchally glad to meet you, and if you don't mind tellin', I'd jis natchally love to know what you'er up to in this neighborhood? The war hain't broke out agin, has it?"

"Now, 'Squire, what suggests war to your mind? I acknowledge that I am very hungry—that is one reason why I wanted to stay all night with you—but I didn't suppose I had begun to look much like an army."

"Oh, by gravy, no; I wouldn't say that you look like an army—especially the *fightin'* part. No; by jacks, I'd never say that. But, honest Injun, now, Colonel; ain't you jis natchally up to some devilment in this neighborhood? Blast my buttons if you ain't the fust white man I've seed from Arkansas since the war. *Gentle*MEN, the way them toothpicks did fight was a caution to General Jackson! Well, Colonel, how er all the folks in Arkansas now, anyhow? Hanged if I wouldn't jis natchally love to know."

" ' 'Squire, that was another reason why I *did* want to stay all night with you. I wanted to tell you all about the folks at home, and talk over old times generally with you. But I reckon I had better get out here under the trees and try to rake enough dry leaves together to make a bed before it gets too dark. And, 'Squire, if I thought you could spare it, and it would not put you to too much inconvenience, I would ask you for a drink of water, for I haven't been as thirsty and *hungry* since the war. But never mind; may be I can stand it till morning. If you *could* spare me a little water, though, and even an ear of corn to parch, I think I could get along much better."

"Confound it, Colonel; shet up that sort er talk! Spare a drink o' water! The Jeemses River! Dog-gone it, go down to the spring and drink a barrelful. And lookee here! By gump, I've knowed fellers to git bit on strangers so bad it made thur heads swim, an' you look to me more like the slickest kind of a yankee carpet-bagger than any Arkansas toothpick I ever seed. But bein' as you *say* you er from Arkansas, an' ain't no kin to old Dave, dog my cats if I don't let you stay, if I never hear the last of it. A year o' corn an' a bed o' leaves! Thunder an' lightnin'; why bless my time, you jis natchally wouldn't need anything else but bristles to be a plum hog. You'll find our fare powerful poor, you will, shore fur a fack, but if you kin put up with it, you er welcome; *provided you ain't after no devilment.*"

While we were unharnessing the team, the 'Squire continued:

"An' you say you ain't no kin to old Dave! Well, I'm jis natchally glad you ain't. I don't say nothin' agin old Davey myself, because I don't know nothin' agin him; but then if the old sinner ever did an honest day's work in his life I've never hearn of it. I don't say nothin' about no distillery, because I don't know nothin' about none, but old Dave jis natchally makes a livin' somehow, an' a mighty good one too, I can tell you. He lives about ten mile from here, and I'm jis natchally glad he don't live no clusser. We ain't got no stills in this neighborhood, and we don't want none. Used to have some, and the woods wuz always full of revenue officers and deputy marshals—deputy devils, I call 'em—prowlin' around makin' trouble, an' the boys jis natchally got discouraged and quit, an' I'm glad they did. We have a mighty good neighborhood here now; nearly all the boys belong to the church. I tell you, doin' away with the stills has jis natchally done us a power o' good; it has, shore for a fack. An you say you live in Arkansas! Gentle*men*, but that's a long ways from here!"

At supper there was nothing in the appearance of the table to suggest starvation, or that the bottom was about to drop out of the country, as the 'Squire seemed to fear.   On the contrary, the fare, though plain, was wholesome and abundant.

The 'Squire's family consisted of himself and wife, and two sons and two daughters, the four latter ranging in age from sixteen to twenty-two years, one of the sons being the oldest and the other the youngest.   Two small rooms constituted his domicile.   The main room contained a large open fireplace at one end and two beds at the other, and also served as a sitting room. The side room served as a dining room and kitchen, and also as the bedroom of the boys.

When bedtime came on the 'Squire asked me if I was a good climber.   I told him I was first rate for a man of my thickness and weight, but that he could see for himself that I was not exactly of the right build for a trapeze performer, and asked him why he wanted to know.   He replied that he would have to send me upstairs to sleep, and was "sorter afeared I couldn't make it, because he had jis natchally never had time to fix reglar steps."

Looking upward, I saw joists overhead, but neither floor nor ceiling.   But to my amazement there was a bed up there, immediately over one of those below, the feet of the bed posts resting upon and toe-nailed to the joists.

The "staircase" consisted of cleats nailed to the wall. Mrs. Beasly and the girls having retired from the room, I proceeded to ascend to my bedchamber by climbing hand-over-hand. As I reached the top cleat and was trying to swing myself up on the joist, the 'Squire called out:

"Think you kin make it? Be kearful; that's right whur a great big Cincinnati drummer was tother night when he fell an' jis natchally lack to have killed hisself; he did, shore fur a fack."

The joists were about three feet apart, with just one narrow plank on them in front of the bed. Sitting down on the side of the bed and drawing off my boots, I tied them together with my handkerchief and swung them across a joist, saddlebag fashion. There were open cracks in the walls, and as I rolled back on the bed and covered up, I heard suppressed giggling in the side room, which threw me into a very profuse cold sweat.

The bedstead was the most abominable contrivance of the kind that I have ever seen. All of its joints were loose and seemed to have been lubricated with rosin. Every time I moved it swayed around and creaked and rattled almost as loud as a Mexican cart.

After I got settled in bed, and probably appeared to be asleep, Mrs. Beasly came quietly back into the room and resumed her seat at the fire with the 'Squire. A moment later I heard her reproaching him for sending me up there. As they were below me and the sounds of their voices ascended, I could hear them even when they conversed in whispers.

"He seems like the nicest kind of a man," I heard the dear old lady say.

"You think he does, do you?" was the suspicious old scamp's response.

"Yes; and Bettie and Susie did so hate for you to put him up there," she replied.

"Bettie and Susie!" he almost snorted. "Well, his looks don't suit me, not a dog-gone bit. An' I want to give you a pinter right now. If he don't fill the bill with the undersigned there musn't be nobody else goin' crazy nor actin' a fool over him about these premises; there musn't, shore fur a fack. I'll bet my years he's up to some devilment, an' if I ketch him lookin' cross-eyed at you or one o' them gals, I'll larrup him until he'll wish he'd never been borned; I jis natchally will."

"Oh, you er too suspicious."

"Well, he may be all right, and then agin he mayn't. He says he's from Arkansas. That's a lie on the face of the papers, as them Asheville lawyers say. What would a feller from Arkansas be doin' in this country, I'd jis natchally love to know. That's too thin. He looks to me mighty like an everlasting revenue officer. An' if he is—IF *he is*, I say—and tries to git down from there to-night to go prowlin' aroun' lookin' for stills, he'll jis natchally break his neck short off at the shoulders. That's why I drove the poor little thing off up there. I reckon you an' the gals would 'a tucked him away in a cradle here by the fire! But I don't want none o' the boys blamin' me for lettin' an enemy roost aroun' my house to pick 'em up unawares. He pretended to be afeared to go on. I jis natchally don't believe that nuther. My opinion is that he did that jis to git to hang aroun' here an' turn your'n an' the gals' heads, until his posse can come in sometime to-night, an' then jis natchally raise sand. Oh, you may depend on it, there's more of 'em in the neighborhood. But the man that can git ahead of old 'Squire Wm. H. Beasly, J. P., will jis natchally have to git up a right smart earlier in the mornin' than I think that feller up there ever riz; he will, shore fur a fack.''

''Aha!'' I said to myself; ''once I was blind, but now I see a thing or two. This grizzly old rascal is a moonshiner, and thinks I am a revenue officer.''

While I was lying there meditating upon the ludi-

crousness of my situation, the girls came tiptoeing back
into the room, and Mrs. Beasly told them to go on to
bed. They came back as noiselessly as kittens to the
bed immediately beneath mine. But not a sound did I
hear, except the faintest rustle of clothing and just a
mere suspicion of persons getting in bed.

I meditated some more. Suppose my crazy old bedstead should break down, or I should get frightened in
my sleep and jump out, or fall out accidentally *and knock
myself cross-eyed!* The 'Squire probably would not
want a better pretext for ''larruping'' me, and the
fact that the old lady regarded me as ''the nicest kind
of a man'' would doubtless add to his enjoyment of the
performance.

Before retiring the 'Squire extinguished the light in
the fireplace, and soon the very stillness of the place
became oppressive to me. Along towards midnight,
and when my nervousness was about to succumb to fatigue and loss of sleep, the dogs began to bark. Some
minutes later I heard a sound as of an owl hooting. I
was satisfied it was a counterfeit. It was a good imita-
tion, but not the genuine sound. I lay still and listened.

The 'Squire arose and tiptoed from the room. The
dogs ceased to bark. Half an hour later the 'Squire
crept back into the room and felt his way back to his
bed.

After the lapse of an hour, and when I was again about to fall asleep, I heard the approach of a cow bell. The dogs barked as before. It was the first time I had ever heard dogs bark at owls and grazing stock. I noticed also that the rattling of the bell was with a somewhat peculiar stroke, and almost as regular as drum-beats. It moved slowly along in front of the house and a short distance beyond ceased entirely. Again the 'Squire stole out for half an hour, and then crept back as before. At the same time I heard his two sons stealthily enter the side room and go to bed, where I supposed they had been all night.

Surely my presence in the neighborhood had put "the boys" on the alert. The 'Squire was evidently sending and receiving "grapevine" dispatches. If questioned about it he would probably say that "the boys" were "jis natchally" holding their usual weekly prayer meeting.

When morning came I felt as if witches had been riding me all night. Wishing to see if the way was clear so that I might arise, I moved my face slightly over the edge of the bed and glanced at the "lower berth," taking particular care, however, that my eyes did not get crossed, because the 'Squire was sitting at the fire, looking as fresh as a morning-glory. To my great relief the girls had arisen and gone from the room.

Seeing me awake the 'Squire remarked that it was
"time to git up." I replied that I was just considering
my ability to *get down*. He chuckled a little over that,
and as I descended he adverted to the topics of the
evening before with the observation:

"An' you say you live in Arkansas! Gentle*men*,
but you er a long ways from home; you air, shore fur a
fack. Well, I'm powerful glad you ain't no kin to old
Dave, anyhow. *I* don't say nothin' agin old Davey
myself, because I don't know nothin' agin him, but
then folks will jis natchally have their suspicions, you
know."

There being no reason why I should conceal my
business from any person, I conceived the idea that
there might be some fun in making it known to the
'Squire. But his eagerness was so great that I determined not to enlighten him directly, but to compliment
Mrs. Beasly by giving her the information first. At
breakfast I purposely engaged her in conversation—not
a cross-eyed conversation, however—and told her truth-
fully who I was, and the nature of my business in that
country. I was correct about the fun. The 'Squire was
both astonished and delighted. The intelligence relieved
him of great suspense and uneasiness, and his cordiality
at once became demonstrative. He said he was "jis
natchally" gladder than ever that I "warnt" no kin to

old Dave.   After breakfast he introduced me to a two-gallon jug, and told his sons—Zeb Vance and Beauregard—to "run and give the Colonel's team a whole lot more feed, and grease his buggy for him."   I declined the first hospitality on the plea that it took but little association with a jug of that size to make me *cross-eyed*, and that I never did like to look cross-eyed at anybody, because I had heard people say it was *bad luck* to do so.

Early that afternoon I got back to Charleston.   Relating my experience at the 'Squire's, I was told that it was a notorious and dangerous moonshine neighborhood, and that he was the chief of the clan—a kind of alcalde among them.   But none of my acquaintances at Charleston had ever heard of old Davey, and I left the country without ever learning why the 'Squire was so glad that I was not related to him.   It may have been due to a factionary feud, the jealousy of a rival leader, or old Dave may have been a fictitious person, and the 'Squire's distrust of him a mere pretense to divert me from "the boys" and stills in his own neighborhood.

My mission in North Carolina was now about fulfilled.   I had been in the State two months, and at Charleston and on the Qualla Boundary, where I had passed most of the time, I had made a great many acquaintances, among both whites and Indians, whom I still remember with much satisfaction.

(2)

Reporting to the Department and asking for further instructions, I received an order by telegraph to return to Washington. Proceeding by way of Asheville and stopping one day at that place, I arrived at Washington on the 15th of December.

CHAPTER V.

FROM WASHINGTON TO THE INDIAN TERRITORY AND
KANSAS—A NIGHT AT TIGER JACK'S—"A DAFE AND
DUMB HAYTHEN NAGUR"—TO THE SAC AND FOX
AGENCY—MY FIRST SPEECH TO BLANKET INDIANS—
TO THE QUAPAW AGENCY—A VISIT TO THE MODOCS.

REPORTING to the Commissioner of Indian Affairs
in person upon my arrival in Washington from
North Carolina, I found him directing the preparation
of instructions for me to proceed to Kansas and the
Indian Territory, to investigate an alleged sale of lands
by the Black Bob Band of Shawnees. It was a case of
unusual importance and the Commissioner was giving
it close personal attention.

Proceeding direct to Muscogee, the seat of the Union
Agency, in the Indian Territory, I arrived there on the
4th day of January. The Union Agency embraces
what are known as the five civilized tribes—the Cherokees, Choctaws, Chickasaws, Creeks and Seminoles.
The Agent at that time was the distinguished young
Cherokee citizen, Colonel Robert L. Owen. Colonel

Owen is part Cherokee, though the white blood largely predominates. He was the first tribal citizen to hold the office of Agent, and he sustained that important and difficult trust throughout his term with distinguished ability and the highest satisfaction and credit to the Government.

Col. Robert L. Owen.

Most of the Black Bobs being under Agent Owen's jurisdiction, and he having recommended the investigation, I was, of course, directed to confer with him for a starting point. Having acquired all the information he could give, on the 7th of January I moved up to Wyandotte, Kansas, and served notice on the alleged purchaser of the land of the time and place when and where I would begin taking testimony.

From Wyandotte I returned by way of Olathe, Kansas, where I stopped a week, to Vinita, in the Cherokee Nation, where I was to begin the investigation, and where I was met by the purchaser and his attorneys.

Nearly all the witnesses being Indians and unable to speak the English language, their depositions had to be taken through an interpreter. When we had taken all the testimony obtainable at Vinita, which took us more than ten days to do, I adjourned the investigation to the Sac and Fox Agency, where I had been informed some important witnesses could be found.

I proceeded by the Frisco Railroad to Red Fork, and thence in a buggy with Mr. C. C. Pickett, who then lived at Sac and Fox. We left Red Fork at sunrise, but there was six inches of crusted snow on the ground, and it so impeded our progress that notwithstanding we crowded our team all day, night overtook us at Tiger Jack's, many miles short of our destination.

Tiger Jack is a full-blood Uchee Indian, and a member of the Creek Legislative Council. He owns a little farm, has a few fruit trees, lives in a comfortable log cabin, and seemed to be traveling "the white man's road" quite successfully. But he pretended that he could neither speak nor understand a word of English, and a grunt was the only response he would make to our request for entertainment for the night, or anything else that we could say to him. A red-headed, scrawny old Irish freighter, whom we happened to meet there, undertook to plead with him in our behalf. He made a very ingenious and eloquent appeal, but when he paused Tiger did not even grunt, but looked as unmoved as the gatepost. In an instant the mettlesome old fellow got mad, and before we could suppress him he had denounced Tiger, among numerous other things, as "a grunting idiot," "a dafe and dumb haythen nagur," and "no gintleman." He even threw off his coat and cap and challenged the Indian to come outside of his yard and fight. But even that failed to move Tiger. Apparently he was no more susceptible of intimidation than he was of persuasion.

But as there was no other house in reach, we made up our minds that if he kept us out of his cabin that night he would at least have to draw a gun on us. Seeing us begin to unharness our team he came outside and motioned to us to drive in under a hayrick in his corral. Then shrugging his shoulders to show us that it was too cold for him to help us, he humped himself up and trotted back into his cabin.

Going in ourselves after feeding the team, we found Tiger sitting before the fire and his wife busy preparing supper for us. Mrs. Jack is also a full-blood Indian, but, having been educated in a mission school, she speaks English without embarrassment. She said Tiger understood English as well as she, but was ashamed to speak it before strangers. We told her jocosely that we had observed his embarrassment before we came in, and had no doubt that he was very bashful in all languages when there was any work to do.

Our supper was bountiful and wholesome, including venison steak and sofka, the latter a delicious dish which the Creeks make of hominy, sweet milk and other ingredients. After a night of perfect rest and refreshing sleep, Mrs. Tiger served us a breakfast which I still remember with a craving appetite.

We arrived at Sac and Fox early in the afternoon, and after I had called on the Agent at his office I received an extremely ceremonious call myself from a committee of the Sac and Fox Council, which I was informed had been in session two days considering a set of by-laws which had been recommended to them by the Department for the administration of justice in the petty domestic affairs of the tribe.   This committee was composed of Keokuk, the principal chief, Pahshepawho, an under chief, and a fussy old fellow whose real name I have forgotten, but whom I heard Henry Jones, the half-breed interpreter, call "Old War Department," a nickname which I considered entirely appropriate. They came, they said, to welcome me in the name of the tribe to their Reservation, and to invite me to address the Council on the proposed code of laws.

Being conducted to the council room by the Agent and the committee, I was introduced, first to the Council and then to the members personally.   The Council was composed of twenty-one members, nineteen of whom were in full Indian costumes. Two members, Chief Keokuk and his son Charley, were in citizens' dress.   Keokuk is the son of the original chief of that name, and for whom the City of Keokuk, Iowa, was named. He is a man of great natural ability and force of character.

After shaking hands all round, I proceeded to speak. I had to speak slowly and pause at the end of each sentence until the interpreter, who stood at my side, could repeat it to the Council in their own language.

Soon after I commenced I felt myself outraged by the conduct of the majority of the Council, but when I dropped the subject of laws and started in to say things to the offending members, I was promptly assured that what I had regarded as gross discourtesy was in fact the very best form of Sac and Fox politeness.

Old War Department occupied a conspicuous seat immediately in front of me, attired in the most fantastic costume of the old-time warrior that I had ever seen. After I had spoken a few sentences, he pulled his blanket up over his head and down in front entirely to the floor, completely wrapping up and hiding every part of his person from sight. I was sure I had started off on a line that did not suit him, and that he had adopted that method of excluding the rest of my speech from his ears, as well as of showing his resentment of what he had already heard.

Apparently following Old War Department's example, another very solemn-looking old fellow arose to his feet, and with great dexterity wound his blanket tightly around his body, from the crown of his head to the soles of his feet, and then stretched himself at full

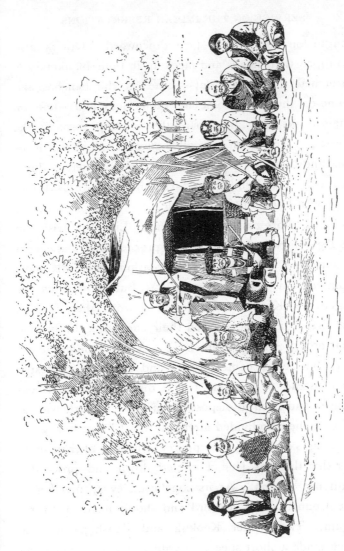

PAHSHEPAWHO AND HIS COUNCILMEN.

length on the bench, face downward. Others also wrapped their heads and faces up in their blankets and stretched themselves out—some on the benches and some on the floor, some on their faces and some on their backs, but all apparently to sleep through the speech. And so on, one after another, all except Keokuk and three or four others settled themselves down in the most undignified and ridiculous postures I had ever seen human beings assume.

It was more than I could stand. Like the Irishman at Tiger Jack's, I got mad and proceeded to make what I considered some very apt quotations from his most pointed and energetic remarks. But as soon as the Agent and Keokuk could get in a word they assured me that I had misconstrued their conduct entirely, and that no disrespect was intended. The offending members themselves came forward and earnestly protested that instead of meaning to be discourteous, their endeavor had been to dispose themselves in such way as to give their undivided attention to all I had to say.

Being satisfied by the apparent sincerity of their manner that this was true, I cooled down and proceeded with my speech. At its conclusion every member of the Council came forward and shook hands with me again. Then, after Keokuk and Pahshepawho had each made a short speech, a vote was taken, which resulted in the adoption of the by-laws by a large majority.

So far as the Black Bob matter was concerned, the trip to Sac and Fox was a disappointment. It turned out that no testimony was obtainable there or in that vicinity that would throw any light on the case one way or the other.

But being now on the ground, I embraced the opportunity to inspect the Agency, as it was my duty to do. Under the jurisdiction of that Agency are the Sac and Fox, Pottawatomie, Iowa and Kickapoo tribes, and the Absentee Band of the Shawnee tribe. Major Moses Neal, of Humboldt, Kansas, was Agent, and I found all of his affairs in reasonably good condition.

From Sac and Fox I went direct to the Quapaw Agency, which is situated in the extreme northeast corner of the Indian Territory. That is an Agency of the remnants of eight different tribes—the Quapaws, Modocs, Wyandottes, Shawnees, Peorias, Ottawas, Miamis and Senecas. Each of these remnants maintains a tribal organization, speaks a different language or dialect, and owns and occupies a separate Reservation. Many of them have made considerable advancement, are self-supporting, and give good hope for future progress. Colonel J. V. Summers, of Missouri, was the Agent, and he seemed to take an intelligent and active interest in their welfare and development.

RESERVATION SCHOOL, SAC AND FOX AGENCY.

The Modocs at the Quapaw Agency are the same Indians that carried on the remarkable war in the lava beds of Oregon in 1873, and whose chief, Captain Jack, killed General Canby. Scar-Face Charley, Captain Jack's brother, who succeeded that noted savage as chief when he was hung for killing General Canby, is still chief of the tribe. This tribe—always small—now numbers but twenty-two adult males, and less than one hundred people altogether.

After these Modocs had been subdued in the lava beds they were brought from Oregon and placed on the Quapaw Reservation, as prisoners of war. They have always been allowed the liberty of the Reservation, but Scar-Face said they had never become reconciled to the Quapaw country, and lived in the hope of being permitted to return some day to their once free and happy homes in the far-off Oregon mountains—a hope, however, which I felt sure, though I had not the heart to tell him, it is their destiny never to realize.

When I had inspected the Quapaw Agency, and taken all the testimony in the Black Bob matter obtainable in that locality, I returned to Muscogee, where I closed the investigation on the 2nd of March.

CHAPTER VI.

MY FINDINGS IN THE BLACK BOB INVESTIGATION—
"SPECULATORS" — AN EX-GOVERNOR, LAWYERS,
BANKERS AND A "PULL" IN WASHINGTON —
$284,000.

MY findings in the Black Bob investigation were
substantially as follows:

In fulfillment of treaty stipulations, the Government,
in 1854, allotted two hundred acres of land in sev-
eralty to each head of a family in the Black Bob
Band.   These allotments were made from the Black
Bob Reservation, which is situated in Johnson County,
between sixteen and twenty-two miles from Kansas
City, and they are now among the most valuable farm
lands in Kansas.

Being in the very midst of the terrible guerrilla war-
fare which began on the Missouri-Kansas border as early
as 1857, and was kept up with unabated ferocity until the
close of the Great Civil War between the States, the
Black Bobs suffered heavily from the devastations of
both sides. Long before the close of that fierce and de-

structive struggle they had been despoiled of all their live stock and other movable property. Finally, to escape from the atrocities of war so frequently happening in their midst, and in which their lives even were imperiled, they abandoned their homes and sought and obtained refuge among the friendly tribes in the Indian Territory.

Between the years 1867 and 1873, the Indians not having returned, and not being expected to ever do so, white settlers took possession of their lands, and have occupied them ever since. This they have done with an honest purpose, and in the confident expectation that the Government would restore the lands to the public domain, subject to purchase or homestead entry by whites, or ascertain by judicial decree who were the heirs of the original allottees, and provide a plan whereby the settlers might purchase direct from them.

No patents had ever been issued to the allottees for their respective allotments, and of course they could make no conveyance to individuals until that was done. But in the meantime nearly all of the original allottees had died. In their cases, of course, patents had to issue, not in their names, but to their heirs or legal representatives. For this reason it was necessary to ascertain and determine by judicial decree who were the heirs of each of the deceased allottees. To provide for this, Congress passed an Act authorizing and directing a suit to be brought in the United States Court at Topeka, to run in the name of the United States against the Black Bob Band of Shawnee Indians. In compliance with this Act the Attorney General of the United States appointed two special assistants, one, a lawyer of Wyandotte, to represent the Government, and the other, a lawyer of Lawrence, to represent the Indians. Both of these attorneys were paid by the Government, each receiving, as I recollect, the sum of $5,000.

The suit was brought and a decree rendered in accordance with the genealogy of the heirs, which the attorney for the Indians had prepared for that purpose. The suit was a mere formality, no resistance being made to any of the proceedings, and the decree being agreed to by both sides. But, however quietly and easily obtained, this decree settled the question of heirships, and perhaps correctly, and the patents were issued accordingly.

But instead of the patents being transmitted to the Indian Agent for delivery to the Indians, as they ought to have been, they were handed over to the attorney for the Government. They were not even intrusted to the attorney for the Indians. The influence of the distinguished United States Senator from Atchison at that time was successfully invoked to thus divert these patents from their proper channel into the possession and control of a man who sustained no friendly relation, either official or professional, to the Indians.

But a conspiracy had been formed to buy the land from under the settlers by any means that could be successfully employed, and an incalculable advantage was to be gained by this unprecedented diversion of the patents.   From the date of their appointment these attorneys had held frequent confidential ·meetings with each other, and with an ex-Governor of Kansas, who resided at Leavenworth.   In fact, their conferences began long before their appointment, and the proof is evident that their plans were laid prior to that time.

Their scheme was to go down into the Indian Territory, hunt up the Indians, and buy the land themselves. The Indians had but a vague idea of their ownership of the land, were totally ignorant of its value, and these "speculators" correctly reasoned that they could secure it for a nominal consideration.   Then, invested with absolute title, they could extort full value from the settlers, and even more, for their respective homes, or compel them to vacate and forfeit all their improvements.

This being their purpose, it would not do, of course, for the Indians to get possession of the patents.   In that case each Indian would know which particular tract belonged to him, and he could sell it to the man who offered him the highest price for it. The settlers would thereby be enabled to compete with the "speculators," and competition must be avoided, even if an unsuspecting and too confiding United States Senator did have to be "pulled" to "work" Indian Commissioner Price. A little matter like that was not to stand in the way of success at all.

In land transactions Indians are slow and capricious, and to make purchases from so large a number, scattered over an area of country two hundred miles in extent, was an undertaking which must have required extraordinary patience and determination. But after two years of persistent efforts, and an outlay of thousands of dollars in the way of expenses, these "speculators" secured deeds to nearly ten thousand acres at $3 per acre.

In consequence of the vacillation and procrastination of the Indians, the Governor and the lawyers had to make a great many trips to different places in the Territory, and in doing so they always traveled together, invariably stopped at the same house, all occupied the same room when practicable, and generally two of them slept in the same bed, and often had what one witness described as "a rattling good time."

The purchases were all made in the name of the Governor, with money furnished by a Leavenworth bank.   The Governor was the sole grantee in each of the deeds.   But whenever an Indian came forward to sign a deed, the attorney for the Indians was on hand with his genealogy of the tribe to see that *all* the heirs to any particular tract joined in the conveyance, and that no money was thrown away on strangers.   And at such interesting moments the attorney for the Government was always present with the patents, and simultaneously with the signing of the deeds the Indians were required to also sign receipts to him for their patents.   But the patents were never in fact delivered to the Indians, but in every instance, except one, they were handed to the Governor.   The exception was in the case of a rather pugnacious young Indian named Billie Williams.   He threatened to break into their room and "whup the whole outfit" if they did not give him his patent.   They gave it to him, paid him $1,000 extra for his two hundred acres, patted him on the back and begged him to say nothing about it.

Notwithstanding the Governor was ostensibly the sole purchaser, it was clear that the attorney for the Indians was always present with his genealogy of the tribe to guard him against the scylla of doubtful heirships, and the attorney for the Government was always there so manipulating the delivery of the patents as to steer him clear of the charybdis of the competition and opposition of the settlers.

No services in the business of buying or selling the land were required of them, or even contemplated, under their appointment from the Attorney General. On the contrary, such services as they were rendering to the Governor were altogether repugnant to the nature of the duties incumbent upon them as attorneys to conduct the lawsuit.

And certainly they were not devoting months and months of their time, and staking whatever of good reputation they may have had, to thus facilitate the Governor to obtain and profit by an undue advantage over both the Indians and the settlers, without reward.

And surely there was room for reward in the prospective profits of the "speculation." Three dollars per acre was the consideration named in each of the deeds—less than $29,000 in all. But upon a personal inspection of the land, as well as from the testimony of competent witnesses, I found it worth from $10 to $35 per acre, or an average of $19.50 per acre, exclusive of the improvements made by the settlers, and an average of $29.40 per acre, or an aggregate of $284,000, including the improvements.

Fortunately a clause in the treaty between the Shawnees and the United States provided that no conveyance by any member of the tribe should be valid until it was approved by the Secretary of the Interior. The deeds in this case were presented at the Department for approval, not by the Governor, the ostensible grantee, himself, but by the attorney for the Government. And *he* did this in writing as attorney for the Governor, and not as attorney for the United States. But before me he testified that he "just happened to be going to Washington to see some Union Pacific Railroad people in New York and Boston, and just carried the deeds along as a gratuitous favor to the Governor because he had free transportation over the railroads and the Governor had not." Evidently forgetting this, the Governor himself testified before me a few days later that he "did not know but that some outside influence might be necessary to procure their approval, in which event he knew this attorney would be the *handiest* man he could get, as he had a political 'pull' in Washington."

Agreeably to my findings as here outlined, I recommended that the deeds be not approved, that the conduct of the attorneys be reported to the Department of Justice, and that they be debarred from practicing before the Department of the Interior.

My recommendation as to the deeds was concurred in by Indian Commissioner Atkins and adopted by Secretary Lamar, and they were never approved. The penalty which this entailed upon the "speculators" was the loss of every dollar that they had "invested" in the "enterprise."

I was never advised what action, if any, was taken in reference to the attorneys; and, as I had performed my duty in the case and was done with it, I never cared to know.

More than a year afterwards, however, the Senator from Wyandotte introduced a resolution into the Kansas State Senate, which was adopted, memorializing the President of the United States to place the State of Arkansas under martial law, because of the assassination of a prominent politician in that State. The Senator from Wyandotte being the attorney for the Government and the man who, the Governor said, had a political "pull" in Washington, the introduction of this resolution reminded me in a characteristic manner that, although he may have been reported to the Department of Justice and debarred from practicing before the Department of the Interior, he was still masquerading in the toga of a State Senator, and guiding the destinies of the Republican party in Kansas as Chairman of the State Central Committee, just as he had been doing for a great many years before.

CHAPTER VII.

TO OKLAHOMA—CLAY COUNTY, TEXAS—TRIP THROUGH
THE COMANCHE RESERVATION — FORT SILL—LONG-
HORN MAVERICK, THE UNPAID HACK DRIVER — HIS
PISTOL PRACTICE FOR PAY DAY.

AT the close of the Black Bob investigation I was
ordered to Oklahoma to expel the intruders
from that much coveted but forbidden country. From
Muscogee I proceeded by rail to Henrietta, Clay
County, Texas.

From Henrietta to Fort Reno, in Oklahoma, a distance of one hundred and fifty miles, the only means of
transportation was the vehicle upon which the mail was
carried, and which I had been informed was a four-
horse Concord stagecoach. But to Fort Sill, seventy
miles, it was a two-horse canvas-covered device of tor-
ture which has been appropriately named "the jerky."

Boarding "the jerky" at Henrietta just at dawn, I
found myself in company with Dr. W. W. Graves, of
Whitesboro, Texas, who was en route to the Kiowa,

Comanche and Wichita Agency to take the place of Agency physician.   He proved to be an agreeable traveling companion.

Clay County was sparsely settled.   Between the Big Wichita and Little Wichita Rivers we passed through a prairie dog town several miles long.   ''The man with the hoe'' had not then made his appearance there very numerously, and the cattle barons seemed to be indeed monarchs of all the range they could ride and all the cattle they could round up.   But it is a magnificent country—entirely too good to be given up to grazing— and since that date settlers have swarmed into it, forcing the maverick lords to yield it up to them and drift further west, or go out of business.

At Charlie's Ford we crossed Red River and entered the Kiowa, Comanche and Apache Reservation.   Thence to Fort Sill our route lay through one of the richest and most beautiful countries that I have ever seen. The first fifteen miles was up the valley of West Cache Creek.   Then crossing a broad, smooth prairie, we entered the valley of East Cache, and followed it to Fort Sill.   It was a splendid spring day, the grass was fresh and luxuriant, and from morning till night there was an unbroken expanse of virgin prairie—rolling ridges, broad valleys, and streams of running water.

Our long day's journey terminated at Fort Sill just

MEDICINE BLUFF, NEAR FORT SILL.

in time for us to hear the boom of the sunset gun and see the flag of our country slowly descend from the tall flagstaff in the center of the parade ground, to be furled for the night and then hoisted again at sunrise.

Fort Sill occupies a picturesque site at the confluence of Cache and Medicine Bluff Creeks, at the eastern extremity of the Wichita Mountains. It was established in 1869, when the Comanches, Kiowas, Apaches, Cheyennes, Arapahoes, Pawnees and Sioux—in fact all the plains Indians—were on the warpath. It is built of blue limestone, contains quarters for ten companies, and is one of the three principal Posts in the Oklahoma and Indian Territories—Fort Reno and Fort Supply being the other two. The permanent garrison consists of four troops of cavalry and three companies of infantry.

At noon the next day we passed Anadarko, the seat of the Agency for the Comanches, Kiowas, Apaches, Wichitas and Caddoes, which is situated on the south bank of the Washita River, thirty-five miles north of Fort Sill.

Dr. Graves stopped at Anadarko, and I thought I was going to have a lonesome trip from there on to Fort Reno, but at the relay station on Spring Creek I got a new driver, who furnished me plenty of amusement. The drivers met there and exchanged outfits, each doubling back on his own drive.

I was struck with the comical appearance, grim humor and droll philosophy of my new driver, and soon became much interested in him. His name, he said, was Longhorn Maverick. He seemed desirous that I should know that driving the mail was not his usual occupation. He said he was a cowboy *by profession*, but being stranded, financially, a few weeks before, he was forced to come down temporarily to driving that old buckboard. It was his intention, he said, to "resign" as soon as he could make the contractor pay him for his labor, and never be caught at that employment again.

Manifestly Mr. Longhorn Maverick had no confidence in his employer, was ashamed of his outfit, and believed that if he ever got any pay for his services he would have to fight for it. He said that in fording the Canadian River as he came down that morning, he drove into a deep hole that had been washed out since the evening before, and got a ducking—in fact narrowly escaped drowning. Then when his team got where he thought they could touch bottom, they came very near getting stuck in quicksand. These accidents, added to other annoyances, present and prospective, had put him in an extremely bad humor. He was sarcastic and sullen, but he looked so exceedingly funny in his sullenness that I could not forbear to play a little on his feelings occasionally

Without our consent we had been transferred at Fort Sill from "the jerky" to an old 'buckboard. This vehicle was so old and dilapidated that no person except an impecunious mail contractor would have acknowledged its ownership. Mr. Maverick told me confidentially that it had descended to the contractor as an "heirloom" from his grandmother. Mr. Maverick also informed me that the contractor was "tainted with aristocracy," and the "heirloom" having been his beloved ancestor's *family carriage*, he prized it as a pearl of great price. He even admonished me that a rule of the contractor required all persons to treat it with the respect and reverence due a relic of such sacred associations, and that every person who disregarded that edict was forever debarred from laying his irreverent hands on the "heirloom," either as passenger or driver. And then in mock emphasis of this admonition, Mr. Maverick irreverently kicked off the remainder of the dashboard, and, drawing his pistol, spitefully shot a spoke out of one of the wheels.

Mr. Maverick had also learned, he said, that the contractor was a very economical man—so economical that he never paid his drivers a cent for their services. This was a rule from which he had never been known to deviate. His trick was to work the drivers as long as he could on promises, and then set them adrift moneyless, threadbare and hungry.

After some reflection Mr. Maverick quietly assured me that other drivers might submit to that sort of treatment if they chose to do so, but whenever he was so constrained to tender his resignation, it would be accompanied by several very pointed personal remarks. In fact, if an honorable exception was not made in his case, *the contractor's son Pete would probably inherit his granny's carriage before the close of the next pay day*. And with that ominous observation Mr. Maverick drew his pistol again and shot out another spoke.

As we trotted down into the broad channel of the treacherous Canadian River, Mr. Maverick looked at me with a peculiar expression from the corners of his remarkably expressive eyes and asked:

"Preacher?"

"Nope.   Why?   Want to get married?" I answered.

"Git married nothin'.   Thought if you was a preacher you'd better be prayin'."

"Anything about to happen?"

"Ninety-nine chances to one there is."

"That's almost unanimous.   Want me to pray for you anyhow?"

"Prayers can't do me no good.   Better be shellin' down the corn for yourself, though."

"What's the difficulty?"

"This blamed river."

"Nice looking river.   What have you against it?"

"Too dad burned unreliable."

"In what respect?"

"Quicksand!   Holes!"

"Bad?"

"Ninety-nine chances to one we'll get stuck, and if we do it would take a hundred yoke of steers to pull us out.   Besides that, we'd sink out of sight in twenty minutes."

"All right.   We'll go in on the one chance in a hundred.   Drive slow, and give your team plenty of time to drink and cool off.   And before you start in, *don't you think this precious old "heirloom" is still incumbered with too many spokes?"*

The expression which this answer produced on Longhorn's face showed plainly that he understood that I knew the really dangerous character of the stream, and was only playing with him.   Giving me only looks for a rejoinder, he plunged in and crowded his team through under whip, and, to our happy surprise, without the slightest mishap.

But the Canadian River is really the most dangerous stream in the Territory.   I had been dreading it, and now finding myself safely across, although not a preacher, it was a relief to me to breathe grateful thanks to the Supreme Protector of all wayfaring mortals for holding us in the hollow of His hand through both the holes and the quicksand.

Longhorn said he would rather go back to Western Texas and live on mezquite beans the balance of his days than be compelled to cross that river every day for a year.

An hour after dark we arrived at Fort Reno, where I found good accommodations with Mr. Evans, the post trader.

CHAPTER VIII.

AT FORT RENO—THE COMMANDING OFFICER AND MY-
SELF A HOPELESS MISFIT—EX PARTE ''CO-OPERA-
TION''— TO OSAGE AGENCY — MOURNING AND
DANCING.

AS stated in the preceding chapter, my business at
Fort Reno was to attend to the expulsion of
cattle and boomers from Oklahoma

What was then known as Oklahoma was the section
of country situated almost exactly in the center of the
Indian Territory, as it then existed, which was opened
to white settlement in 1889, and from which the Counties of Oklahoma, Cleveland, Kingfisher, Canadian,
Logan and Payne have since been formed.

Being owned by Indians it was not subject to settlement or occupancy by whites. But the Indians did
not occupy it themselves—having relinquished that
right to the Government years before—and whites had
now invaded it, and were grazing cattle and making
settlements, regardless of the law.

It had been reported to the Department that there

were several hundred of the invading settlers, or boomers, as they were called, and fifty thousand head of the intruding cattle.   My orders were to notify these intruders to vacate by a given day, and to call on the commanding officer at Fort Reno to send troops to evict all boomers who failed to obey, and drive out all cattle not removed by the owners.

The commanding officer at Fort Reno had been furnished with copies of my orders, and ordered to cooperate with, and aid and assist me to carry them out. These orders were not free from ambiguities and apparent contradictions, but as I alone was responsible for their execution, Major Emile Adam, whom I found temporarily in command, left the construction of them entirely to me, with the cordial assurance that he stood ready to respond to any call that I might make on him for troops.

Major Adam agreed with me that the only practicable plan consistent with my orders was the one which I had adopted.   Captain J. M. Lee, of the Army, who was at the time in charge of the contiguous Reservation of the Cheyennes and Arapahoes as Acting Agent, and with whom I was directed to confer for advice and information, also concurred in my plan.   Indeed my recollection is that he suggested it to me and commended it to Major Adam.

(3)

But before any step had been taken, except publication of notice to the intruders, Colonel E. V. Sumner, the permanent commanding officer, who had been absent at Fort Leavenworth, returned to the Post and resumed command. His arrival was signalized by an instantaneous cessation of co-operation between the commanding officer and myself. It was demonstrated to my satisfaction in my first interview with him, though a brief one, that there would be no co-operation or harmony between us. It was apparent that as co-operators we were a hopeless misfit. Disapproving the plan which I had adopted he refused to assist me to carry it out. On the other hand, the plan which he proposed was more heroic than was permissible under my orders, as I understood them, and also, as I thought, unnecessarily harsh on the intruders. For that reason I could not sanction it, or suffer it to be enforced on my responsibility. It soon became manifest that our disagreement was irreconcilable. Telegraphing that information to the Department, I asked to be relieved from further service in the matter, which was promptly done, and I was ordered on to Osage Agency.

During my stay at Fort Reno I became pleasantly acquainted with Captains A. E. Woodson and E. M. Hayes, Lieutenant A. C. Macomb, and several other officers, from each of whom I received courteous atten-

tions.   They all told me that "co-operation" between
Colonel Sumner and myself was altogether unlike the
usual "co-operation" between him and themselves.
Being their commanding officer, it was his habit, they
said, to require of them a prodigious amount of the only
kind of "co-operation" that he seemed to know anything about.   "Co-operation" between him and myself
was of a strictly negative kind—a case, possibly, of extreme stubbornness on both sides.   But as between him
and them, "co-operation" partook much less of the
nature of a "deadlock."   It was more *ex parte*, it
must be confessed, but it was also much more expedi-
tious.   They said that when he said "co-operate" to
them they always dropped everything else and "co-op-
erated" with him right there on the spot, and generally
in double-quick time.   They said the "privilege" of
doing this was about the only one they had that was
not liable to be denied them any day, and they appre-
ciated it, because the surgeon had often advised them
that it might impair their health to dwell permanently
in the guardhouse.

Proceeding by way of Caldwell and Arkansas City,
Kansas, I arrived at Osage Agency while all the Indians
on the Reservation were in camp there, awaiting an
annuity payment.   The Agent had recently assumed
charge of the Agency, and it was soon manifest to me

that his friends had made a great mistake in procuring his appointment. He had been colonel of a regiment of Michigan cavalry during the war, and commanded a brigade in one of the Virginia campaigns, in which he distinguished himself for skill and gallantry. At that time, and for many years afterward, he doubtless possessed great mental vigor and executive ability. But he had never had experience in the management of Indians, and was now too old to learn. Indeed he was too much enfeebled, both physically and mentally, by age and ill-health, to have properly discharged the duties of Agent, even if he had known how.

The Osages are not refractory Indians, but they had not been slow to detect either the lack of experience or the infirmities of age, and by wheedling and encroachment, had just about taken charge of both the Agency and the Agent. He had suffered them to camp all around his house. Not less than one hundred and fifty tepees were crowded against his yard fence. Inhabiting these tepees were at least seven hundred and fifty Indians, and an equal number of dogs.

It was also the mourning season of the Osages—a time when all the tribe, at regular hours during a certain number of days, mourn for all who have died during the preceding year. But the reader must not get the impression that these periodical seasons of mourning ever interfere with the dancing season, which comes in with the new year and goes out with the old, or, in other words, is perpetual. The terrible wail of the mourner is heard only once a year, except when a death occurs, but the sound of the tom-tom may be heard somewhere on the Reservation every day in the year.

Those who had domiciled themselves as neighbors of the Agent were doing their full duty at both mourning and dancing. Both "exercises" seemed to be conducted by an established programme, with Chief Black Dog as master of ceremonies.

At dark the tom-toms were brought out and the dancing commenced, and blended with the monotonous tom-tom of the drums, and the merry ki-yi of the dancers, were the fighting and barking of the dogs.

This was kept up until midnight, and, as the reader may imagine, while it continued sleep was impossible in the Agent's house or any where near it.

At 3 o'clock the mourning began, and then it seemed that pandemonium had broken loose in earnest. The uproar was started by a few crones—professional mourners—but in ten minutes all the Indians and dogs in camp had joined in and were wailing and howling as if the judgment day was at hand. This was continued half an hour or more, and then the camp became comparatively quiet until daylight.

At daybreak the squaws commenced coming to the hydrant in the Agent's yard to fill their water pails, and then there was no more rest for the weary, or sleep for the sleepy. Then when the Agent's family sat down to their meals enough of his wards flattened their noses against the windows to almost exclude the daylight from the dining room.

This had been the situation of the Agent and his family for three or four days when I arrived, and it had driven him almost to distraction. He said he had suffered the Indians to thus intrude upon his premises because, being a new Agent, he wanted to show them that he felt a paternal interest in their welfare and happiness, and would even sacrifice his own comfort and that of his family to promote theirs. I expressed my approval of his motives, and forbore to criticise his judgment except to mildly suggest that he probably could have made even a more favorable impression by taking fifteen or twenty families into his house as guests.

The truth is I pitied the unfortunate old man in his troubles, and proffered, purely as a favor to him, because it was not my duty, to make the Indians move their camp myself. But, notwithstanding he was worried almost to desperation, he was afraid it would impair his influence over them even for me to take action.

Of course, without the slightest doubt of the Agent's honesty, in the light of this error of judgment, and other evidences of incapacity and want of tact, I could not be hopeful of his success.   Nevertheless, I was determined to do my duty by him.   I made a thorough inspection of his Agency, instructed him as far as practicable in regard to his duties, and made such recommendations to the Department as I thought would facilitate him in the administration of his affairs.

CHAPTER IX.

ORDERED TO OURAY AGENCY, UTAH, "FORTHWITH"
—UP THE KAW AND GREAT SMOKY HILL VALLEYS
—IN DENVER—IN CHEYENNE—A SYMPATHIZING
PORTER—AT GREEN RIVER, WYOMING—ALARMING
NEWS OF THE SITUATION AT OURAY.

ON the 12th of June I received an order by telegraph to proceed *forthwith* to Ouray Agency, Utah, where I would find written instructions awaiting me.

To say that I was pleased with this order would be to express but half the truth. I was elated. I had always wanted to visit the beautiful City of Salt Lake, and see my Mormon brother under his own vines and fig trees. I use the plural number because I had always understood that he had several, and sat around under them quite promiscuously.

I had heard of no disturbance at Ouray, and the order did not create even a suspicion in my mind that there might be trouble there with the Indians. I supposed the emergency was merely a business matter.

Striking the railroad at Arkansas City, Kansas, I ran up to Kansas City, and there took the early morning train west on the Kansas Pacific. That road follows the valleys of the Kaw and Great Smoky Hill Rivers— two of the richest valleys in the world—and from morning till night we were in the midst of a vast sea of corn and wheat fields. It was wheat harvest time, but the corn was not yet in tassel, and a prettier landscape than those alternating deep-green corn fields and golden wheat fields would indeed be hard to find.

I was greatly interested all day in the work of the harvesters. From the car windows I saw scores of great self-binding reapers, and combined reapers and threshers, at work in the fields. Those magnificent combined reapers and threshers are propelled through the fields by steam, cutting the grain in front and rolling it off in sacks at the rear.

The weather having been intensely hot at Osage, and expecting to be on duty in that part of the country all summer, I had discarded all of my heavy clothing, and fitted out with a straw hat, alpaca coat, and other garments to match.

And now as we thundered along through Eastern and Central Kansas under the hot June sun it was easy to see that I was the most comfortably dressed man on the train. I supposed that all the other passengers were tenderfeet from the North and East, as they were sweltering in rather heavy, dark clothes, and often during the day I noticed many of them regarding my soda water costume with evident envy. Even when I sought my berth in the sleeper and retired for the night, away out toward the west line of the State, my clothes were still in season. When I arose at 6 o'clock the next morning we were running through an arid plain in Colorado. There was not a tree in sight—no vegetation of any kind, in fact, except some scattering bunch grass and sagebrush. The Rocky Mountains were in sight, and away off to the southwest snow-capped Pike's Peak stood out clear and distinct against the horizon. We were in three hours run of Denver.

All the passengers being up, I again observed that mine were the only straw hat, alpaca coat and summer trousers on the train. I also realized that we had climbed up into a different climate. We were now at an elevation of perhaps three thousand five hundred feet above Kansas City. A fire was burning in the heater furnace in the car, and I noticed that some of the passengers had on overcoats.

I went out on the rear platform to try the temperature. There was a strong wind from the north, and it took me but a minute to discover that if I stood out there very long I would get frost-bitten.

From that time on it seemed to me that all the passengers stared at my picnic attire, and winked and said things to one another on the sly, more than was necessary or polite, and I was glad when we got to Denver, where I hoped I would see no more of any of them.   I was now satisfied that they were not as "tenderfooted" as they at first seemed to be.

We arrived in Denver at 9 o'clock, and had to lay over there four hours.   By that time of day the sun was warm enough for me to take a walk over the city.

Denver is indeed the Queen City of the Rocky Mountains.   Situated between the Great Plains on one side and the Rocky Mountains on the other, and at an elevation of five thousand five hundred feet above the sea, the atmosphere there is so pure and clear that objects can be seen at long distances with wonderful distinctness. The mountains are said to be fifteen miles away, and yet from the centre the city appears to be built right up against them.

At 1 o'clock my train pulled out for Cheyenne, Wyoming.   The railroad skirts the plains all the way from Denver to Cheyenne, but the Rocky Mountains may be distinctly seen from the car window at any point on the route.

The road crosses the South Platte River at the town of Greeley, where the entire valley seems to be under irrigation. Great canals take the water from the river and conduct it along the foothills for miles and miles down the valley, giving it out on the way to lateral ditches, which distribute it among the farms.

At the Greeley depot I saw large quantities of fruits and vegetables, including strawberries of very fine size and quality—so fine indeed that I accused one of the venders of having imported them from Arkansas. He denied it, however, and turned the laugh on me by the remark that he had "never heard of that place before!"

We arrived at Cheyenne at 5 o'clock, and stopped there more than an hour to get supper and transfer to the main line of the Union Pacific from Omaha to San Francisco.

Cheyenne is nearly a thousand feet higher than Denver, and, it seemed to me, more than a thousand feet colder. I started up town, but soon found that I could not stand it without an overcoat, and was attracting too much attention anyhow. So I returned to the sleeping car, where I was glad to find the porter shoveling coal into the heater furnace. As I walked in he glanced sidewise at me and said:

"Hits guine ter be mighty cole up dar under dem snow sheds whar de road crosses de mountain."

And we were going up into the snow, eh! That was information to me, though I did not feel called on to say so. On the contrary I said:

"Yes; I've no doubt it will. Will we get there before bedtime?"

"Oh, yass, sah; *befo' dark.* Big, helty man lak you couldn't go to bed dat early. But den dat's all right, boss. I's on to dem close o' yourn, an I'll fire up and make dem udder fellers take off dere coats an set in dere shirt sleeves wid you. Dem 'ud be mighty proper close in New Aurleens. I speck dis de fuss time you ebber come out Wes'. I wish I'd nebber come out yere de fuss time. Dis de poores' white man's country I ebber did see. I'se guine back to Arkansas, whar I come from, de berry fuss chance I git. Dat what I sholy guine do. I'd give fo' bits right now fur one dem Hot Springs baffs to wash dis akkerli duss offer me."

"Hold on there. Are you from Arkansas?"

"Lookee yere, boss, you'se not a dipity sheriff, is you?"

"No; and if I were I wouldn't arrest a nigger that kept a good fire for me. But I am from Arkansas, and thought perhaps we might be related."

"De Lordy mussy, boss, I speck we is. You know Colonel Beaver Dam Williams, what owns dat big plantation down on Nobles' Lake?"

"Oh, yes."

"Does you, shore enough? Why, de Lordy mussy,

boss, me an de Colonel been runnin' togedder ebber since I been big enough to tote a letter to de pos' office. De Colonel's one mighty good white man; dat what he sholy am. Say, boss; you right suttin you'se not a dipity sheriff?''

"Oh, yes; positive.''

"Is you? Lor' bless you fur dat! I ain done nothin', but I never did lak to 'sociate wid a dipity sheriff. Dars a yaller gal at Pine Bluff been makin' her brags she guine ter hab me brung back dar wid a breach o' promises, but I ain' make no more promises den she is, an if she keeps goin' on erbout it I guine ter hab her brung out yere and gib her tc dem Mormon niggers at Ogden. Dat what I guine do. While I was stop dere de udder day dey tole me dey mighty short on wives. Dey ain' got more'n three or fo' apiece, an dem white Mormons dey tells 'em dat ain' half enough. You hear my horn, if she dat bad off to marry, I jis take her ober dar and lef' her. You know dem Mormon niggers, dey'll jis marry all de wimmin dey can git dere hans on. Boss, lemme git some more coal in dat furnis. I'll make dem udder fellows sweat 'fo' dey gits through dem snow sheds, I sholy will. I'll make em wish dey didn't hab on nothin' but linen dusters. I doan lak dere looks much, nohow. Dere ain' a drummer in de whole shootin' match. Dere ebbery

one two-risses.   We calls 'em two-risses because a heap
o' times hit takes two of 'em to pay de porter a dime.''

As the train pulled up to the station at Green River
the next morning, Indian Inspector Robert S. Gardner,
with whom I was acquainted, came elbowing his way
through the crowd to meet me.   He said he intuitively
knew when he saw the situation at Ouray that I would
be the man sent to take charge!

''Take charge?   What is the matter down there?''
I asked as my mind ''forthwith'' reverted to home and
the gleefulness with which I had received the order.

''Why, don't you know?   What are your orders?''
the Inspector asked.

''I know absolutely nothing,'' I replied.   ''My order
is simply to repair 'forthwith' to Ouray and find instructions.   I am going in blindfolded, as it were.''

I may as well confess that I was about to become
''forthwith'' somewhat dissatisfied with the service.

''Well,'' the Inspector continued, ''you'll find plenty
of 'instructions' down there—enough to make your head
swim.   In addition to what you get from the Department, Saponero and Colorow will want to give you 'a
whole passel,' and you'll find about as much comfort
in one as in the other.   The Indians are mad and
threatening.   The Agent telegraphed his resignation
the other day, and immediately lit out for tall timber,

without waiting for leave from the Department.   I was down there a week ago, and the Indians, whom I have known personally for years, would not speak to me.   I remained one night and hurried back to report the situation to the Department.   The War Department had also heard of the trouble, and Colonel Bush, of the Sixth Infantry, was there with a small escort from Fort Douglass the same night I was, to ascertain the situation.   He pushed right back, and troops will be sent as quick as possible.   It will be your duty to try to pacify the Indians and prevent an outbreak until troops can go to your relief.   W. A. McKewen, the Agency Clerk, a brave young fellow from Baltimore, is in charge, with nine white employes, but they are liable to be attacked any day.''

I felt very tired, and sat down on a bench to rest.

CHAPTER X.

THE DRUGGIST AT GREEN RIVER—ONE HUNDRED AND
SIXTY MILES ACROSS MOUNTAINS, DESERTS AND
"BAD LANDS"—A MORMON OASIS—ARRIVED AT
OURAY AGENCY.

MY arrival at Green River being on Sunday I had to
lay over there until Monday before I could get
transportation to Ouray.

Green River is a small town, and devoid of beauty,
but during the day I discovered that it contained a
number of extremely picturesque citizens.   In a drug
store I called for some quinine.   Judging from the appearance of the proprietor, who was alone in the store,
I should have set him down as an ox driver, and I was
afterwards told that he had in fact been an ox driver,
and also a miner, a sheep herder, a justice of the peace,
a ranch boss, county judge, chairman of a vigilance
committee, member of the Legislature, and a section
foreman on the railroad.   He had a good store, but it
was evident that he knew nothing about the business,

and could not weigh or measure medicines with a smaller implement than a spade or a quart cup. He said he kept a young doctor about the store to measure out all the "pizen medicines," but as quinine was not "pizen," he guessed he and I could get it ourselves, without waiting for the doctor, who happened to be absent. Then handing me a bottle, he told me to help myself.

"All right," I said; "give me some capsules to put it in."

"Capsules?" What's them, pardner?" he asked.

I explained what they were, and he said:

"Oh! *Them things?* Great gulliver! A drummer sneaked in here while I was off on the round-up last fall, and fooled Dock into buyin' four bushel of 'em. Dock thought he had played thunder, and sure enough he had, for when they come we found out they wus a fraud, and throwed 'em away. You don't want none o' them things. You couldn't fill a dozen of 'em in two days."

"Oh, they are not hard to fill," I replied, "and I don't want the quinine unless you have them."

"Sorry you said not hard to fill," he returned, "but hold on a minute. I believe we throwed 'em back here. I jis want to show you what a whole passel you don't know about 'em."

At the place indicated in a rear corner I saw a great

pile of sweepings from the floor. Scratching around in this pile of dirt, he got out an armful of capsule boxes and piled them on the counter. Opening a box, I commenced filling the little cups by tapping the open ends down on the quinine. The druggist was amazed. Watching me closely until I had filled three or four, he suddenly straightened up and exclaimed:

"Say, pardner! If you ever hear of the fool-killer driftin' over into this part of the range, jis give me and Dock a signal, will you, and by grab we'll hide out. Me and him tried to fill them things with a spoon!"

From Green River I had the company of Mr. Sam McDowell, a very intelligent young man who was returning from a visit to his home at Danville, Kentucky, to Ouray Agency, where he was a clerk in the trader's store.

Our route the first day lay across a hot and dusty sagebrush plain. The early morning was cool and bracing, but by 9 o'clock the heat was intense. The sun blazed on us from above, and was reflected back in our faces with increased heat from the garish earth below. All day we could see vast snow-banks glistening in the sunlight on the high mountains off to the south and west of us. But the sight of those ice-clad peaks in the distance only tantalized us, instead of alleviating our discomfort there on that hot and shadeless plain. Just before night we reached Maxon's ranch, the first settlement from Green River.

Next morning we passed through Seger Canyon, in which we found the heat more insufferable than it was on the plain the day before. Escape from the sun was just as impossible, and between the bare walls of the canyon there was not a breath of air stirring. At noon we crossed over to the west side of Green River at Jarvey's Ferry.

Soon after crossing the river we began to ascend the Uintah Mountains, which lay directly across our road, and an hour before sunset we drew wearily up to the Diamond Ranch, a summer sheep ranch on the summit of Diamond Pass, at an elevation of perhaps twelve thousand feet.

Next morning I was shown ice more than an inch thick. And that was no unusual circumstance. Owing to the great elevation ice forms there an inch thick in the warmest nights of the year. About the 1st of October the pass fills up with snow, and remains so until about the 1st of May. When it was thus closed all the mail for Uintah and Ouray Agencies and the town of Ashley had to be carried over by footmen on snowshoes—the only means by which a crossing could be effected.

Resuming our journey at sunrise in two hours we had

descended from the mountain and entered a stretch of
country unlike any I had ever seen before.   It wore a
most forbidding aspect, and was appropriately named
"the bad lands."   There was not a tree, scarcely a blade
of grass, no vegetation of any kind, no sign of moisture,
no rocks—nothing but round little clay hills and hollows.
All places and all sides looked alike.   The surface of
the earth from the bottom of the hollows to the tops of
the hills was everywhere precisely the same—alternating
streaks of dun, yellow and red clay, and all baked and
cracked like the silt in the bed of a dry lake.

Winding, twisting and toiling up and down and
around those hills and hollows until 12 o'clock, we then
emerged from the "bad lands" and entered the valley
of Ashley River, at the town of Ashley.   This valley is
a real oasis—the only one on the road between Green
River and Ouray.   It is two or three miles wide, six or
seven long, and at that time contained about 2,500 in-
habitants, all Mormons.   The main settlement constituted a very pretty little rural town, and throughout
the valley there were many evidences of thrift and in-
dustry.   A good portion of the valley was under irrigation, and interspersed among the fields of grain and
alfalfa were orchards and long lines of shade trees,
which added greatly to the natural beauty and attract-
iveness of the valley.

After halting an hour and a half at Ashley, we started out on the last twenty-five miles of our journey. Ascending from the valley, we saw our road stretching away to the south across the sandiest, hottest and most desolate desert that we had yet encountered. A few miles further on we crossed the boundary line, and entered the Reservation.

In this blazing desert there was neither shade, nor water, nor human inhabitant, and but little of either vegetable or animal life of any kind—scarcely anything but deep, loose sand, into which our horses sunk to their fetlocks at almost every step. The poor beasts staggered in the traces almost overcome by the heat.

And although McDowell and I were protected from the direct rays of the sun by the hack cover, being unaccustomed to such exposure, we suffered almost as severely as the horses. Our heads ached, our eyes became inflamed, and our faces burnt and swollen.

An hour after dark we arrived at the Agency.

CHAPTER XI.

IN CHARGE OF OURAY AGENCY——HOW A CLERK HAD
   ROBBED THE INDIANS — THE AGENT ''NO MORE
   WRITE,'' BUT PAID THE MONEY ''PURTY QUICK,''
   AND RESIGNED BY TELEGRAPH——TROOPS EXPECTED.

IN the letter of instructions referred to in the telegraphic order at Osage, and which I found awaiting
me at Ouray, I was informed of the Agent's abdication,
and ordered to take charge of the Agency myself, pacify the Indians, if possible, and keep the Department
advised of the situation.

As soon as I had read the letter I sat down at a desk
in the Agent's office and wrote an order formally assum-
ing charge, and then immediately addressed myself to
an inquiry into the character of the Indians and the
causes of the threatened outbreak.

The Indians of the Ouray Agency number about
1,200 persons, and are known as the Uncompahgre
Band of Utes. They are among the most benighted
and intractable savages in the United States.. At that

date there were but two members of the band who could speak English well enough to carry on a simple conversation. Saponero was principal chief and Colorow an under chief.

These Indians had formerly lived in Colorado, and in their treaty of removal to Utah they had expressly reserved the right to return to their old Reservation at certain seasons of the year, to hunt. But lately a fight had occurred on White River between Colorow's band and some cattlemen, who had accused the Indians of stealing cattle, and forbidden them to ever cross the line of the old Reservation again. This had caused great irritation and excitement among the Indians, and as they were angrily asserting their right and intention to continue to hunt in the forbidden country, further trouble was liable to occur any day. And, of course, a serious collision with the whites in that quarter would be immediately followed by an uprising at the Agency.

The two Reservations, the old and the new, lie broadside to each other, and are only separated by the boundary line between Colorado and Utah. On the Colorado side are certain streams and valleys which the Indians have always coveted, and which were formerly thought to be in Utah. The Indians say that while the tribe lived in Colorado they were always told that those streams and valleys were not in that Reservation, but in Utah. Indeed they say that at the time of the treaty of removal the Treaty Commissioners themselves told them that they were in Utah, and would fall within their new Reservation in that Territory. I have no doubt that was true, for at that time they *were* in Utah, as the boundary line was then recognized. But since the removal of the Indians the discovery had been made by a careful resurvey that the boundary line was in fact several miles west of the original survey, and that the coveted streams and valleys were *not* in Utah, but in Colorado—not in the new Reservation, but in the old one.

Of course this was not a piece of legerdemain to defraud the Indians, but they believed it was. In fact from their standpoint, and with their benighted vision, they could see it in no other light, and no proof or argument could convince them to the contrary. To them it was a hard materialization, and on a large scale, of the fabled proposition of the white man to the Indian at the close of a day's hunt:

"I'll take the turkey, and you take the buzzard; or *you* take the buzzard, and *I'll* take the turkey."

They said: "When we lived in Colorado the white man told us that strip of country did not belong to us— was not in our Reservation. He used to show us the line and forbid us to cross over. Then he asked us to 'swap' countries, and told us that when we came over here those running waters and grassy valleys would be ours. We came, and the white man took possession of our old Reservation. Then, the first thing we knew, the white man snatched those streams and valleys away from us—took them out of our new Reservation, where they had always been, and put them in the old, where they had never been before—and say, 'white man mistaken; they do not belong to Indian, but to *him!*' All time belong to *white man!*''

I asked Mr. McKewen who they accused of this. He replied:

"Me, sir! Washington. Everybody. The first time you hold a pow-wow with them they will charge you with it."

I also asked him if he thought they would fight over the disputed strip and the right to hunt in the old Reservation. He said:

"Yes, sir. Colorow is over there now with his band, making medicine, dancing, and swearing that if he is interfered with he will kill off the entire "tribe" of white people. He has never seen but a few thousand whites, and he cannot believe that they outnumber the Utes more than two or three to one, at most, and he considers one Ute equal to several white men. Moreover, Saponero has lately gone up DuChesne valley and built a wickiup right across the west boundary line, or right across where he thinks it is, and is living there to keep us from stealing that side of the Reservation also.''

And this was not all.   Contemporaneously with these occurrences a large sum of money was sent to the Agent with which to make an annuity payment.   After all the Indians on the Reservation had presented themselves and received their shares, there were three hundred and sixty names on the rolls still unpaid.   The Agent and Clerk McKewen had both lately come to the Agency.   The census of the tribe had been taken, and the pay-rolls made out and certified, by their predecessors, and they were alike unfamiliar with the papers and unacquainted with the Indians.   They read off the three hundred and sixty names to the Indians present, through the interpreter, and inquired where the delinquents were, and the cause of their absence.   The Indians answered that every member of the tribe had been paid, and that the unpaid names were fictitious. They also claimed the remainder of the money—$3,600 —for themselves, and demanded that it be paid to them at once.   The Agent was convinced that the names were fictitious and fraudulent, but under the regulations of the Department he was required to return the money to the Treasury until the roll could be corrected for the next payment, and he so explained to the Indians. They retired to hold a council.

In a short while a delegation of chiefs came back to the office and inquired if money had been drawn on the fictitious names at any previous payment. The retained copies of the pay-rolls on file in the office, which were hurriedly examined, showed that they *had* been paid equally with the *bona fide* names—$10 per capita— at each payment for several years past, and the chiefs were so informed. With suppressed rage they returned to the council and reported their information. It was received with furious grunts of anger, and provoked several highly inflammatory speeches. The speakers said they had seen the white man steal their eastern boundary, and been shot at on their old Reservation, where they had a right to be, but they had not known that a part of their annuity was also being stolen from them. It was time to fight!

The whole tribe reappeared at the office and again demanded the money. The Agent started to explain again that he would first have to write to Washington for authority to pay them. Jerking out their guns and pistols, and cocking them in the faces of the Agent and clerk, they commanded in most belligerent tones:

"*No more write!!! Money! Purty quick!! Pay it!!!*"

And the Agent "no more write." He counted the money out to them "purty quick," and the next thing he wrote was his resignation, and the employes used to laugh and tell me that he did that *by telegraph*, and followed it up in person an hour later on the best horse at the Agency.

Subsequent investigation developed proof that the robberies had been committed by the former clerk without the knowledge of his Agent, the latter's responsibility for them consisting solely in his incompetency and neglect of duty.

Under the regulations of the Department the Agent is required to take a census of his Indians once a year, and correct and certify the roll for each annuity payment, by adding the births and subtracting the deaths. Then when the money is sent to him it is his duty to divide the total amount by the whole number of Indians, to ascertain the per capita share of each, and make payment accordingly.

But the former Agent at Ouray being an easy-going, incompetent man, he had intrusted all this business to the clerk, who had promptly embraced the opportunities thus afforded to rob the Indians. Being permitted to take the census and make the disbursements in his own way, he was enabled to enter the three hundred and sixty fictitious names on the rolls and draw their per

capita shares and forge their receipts therefor at each
payment, without detection by the stupid interpreter or
the two unsuspecting and incompetent white witnesses
required by the regulations.   And the pay-rolls being
perfect on their face, it was impossible for the accounting officers at Washington to detect the fraud.

After making out the rolls for the payment just described, this clerk was unexpectedly dismissed from the
service, and knowing that exposure, and perhaps arrest
and punishment, would follow, he immediately de-
camped for Mexico.   And before the payment came
on the Agent was also removed.

And a few days subsequent to this mutiny the Indians
were aroused to another dangerous tumult of anger and
excitement by an unusual double tragedy among themselves.   A common Indian named Arrowod shot and
killed a prominent chief and medicine man named
Shavanaw, while the latter was sitting on his pony, on
the plaza immediately in front of the Agent's office,
surrounded by a score of his warriors.   After shooting
Shavanaw, Arrowod wheeled to ride away, but before
he could get out of range the friends of his victim had
fired a hundred bullets into his body.   A rope was then
tied around his feet and his body dragged to the bank
of DuChesne River by his own pony.   At the river
the pony was also shot, and its lifeless body and that of

its owner, securely lashed together, were, amidst the most ferocious yells of anger and the wildest howls of grief, rolled over the bank into the deep and turbid river by the savage chief's savage avengers.

Following these disturbances, and just before my arrival, an Indian named Paprice was killed by another named Wass. Wass was a head man and "medicine man," and, I think I may add, a bad man. He was accused by Paprice of having made "bad medicine" for his two sons, both of whom had recently died. Meeting Wass, Paprice said to him:

"You have killed both of my pappooses, and you might as well kill me."

From a motive known only to himself, Wass raised his gun and shot the old man dead. When called to account for this deed the only justification that Wass or his friends had to offer for it was that as Paprice was rather an old man he had only a few more years to live anyhow, and that, therefore, no very great wrong had been done. Indeed, for this reason he and his friends regarded the very suggestion of punishment as preposterous.

This was the state of affairs that had constrained the Agent to resign and abandon his Agency, and inspired the telegraphic order to me to proceed "forthwith" to take his place.

And this was not only the condition of the Uncompahgres, but two other large bands of Utes on the adjoining Reservation—the Uintahs and White Rivers—were similarly disaffected. They had lately set fire to the Agency farm fence, backed the Agent up in a corner of his office, kicked him, jammed his hat down over his eyes, subjected him to other gross indignities, and committed other acts of insubordination.

CHAPTER XII.

HOW THE GOVERNMENT SERVICE IS CONDUCTED AT
THE AGENCIES—DESCRIPTION OF OURAY—THE EM-
PLOYES—AN IMPOSING SAVAGE ARRAY—ARRIVAL
OF THE INDIANS FOR A COUNCIL.

IN the beginning all of the tribes roamed at will over
the vast domain of the West.   Boundary lines were
unknown to them.   All were free to go wherever their
fancy led them, and it is known that some of them,
notably the Comanches, hunted and raided from the
British Possessions on the north into Central Mexico on
the south.   I have myself often been told by old
Comanche warriors of their visits to the Dakotas at the
British line, and of their raids into Mexico, where the
trees swarmed with monkeys and parrots.

But sending out Commissions from time to time to
make formal treaties with the various separate tribes,
the Government finally settled them all down on comparatively small Reservations, and established Agencies
for their management and control.   In these treaties
the Indians relinquished their right to roam over the

(4)

OURAY AGENCY, UTAH.

country at large, accepted their respective Reservations, and covenanted to dwell within their boundaries, and learn to walk in the white man's road.

In consideration of these concessions on the part of the Indians, the Government covenanted on its part to pay them an annuity in cash, or subsistence supplies, until they could learn to support themselves—generally limited to twenty, twenty-five and thirty years; to provide mills, shops and medicines to meet their necessities; an Agent and teachers to govern them and teach them the arts of civilization, and a physician to attend their sick.

Ouray was established in fulfillment of one of these treaties.   It was built for a temporary army post, and after having been abandoned by the War Department it was turned over to the Interior Department for an Agency.   All the houses, except the Agent's dwelling and one other, are mere huts, constructed of logs set in the ground stockade fashion, the roofs made of dirt, and the cracks daubed with mortar.

It is situated at the confluence of the Green and DuChesne Rivers, in one of the wildest, most isolated and remote regions in the West.   The two nearest white settlements were Uintah Agency and the Mormon town of Ashley, each twenty-five miles distant.   The next nearest were Rangely, Colorado, sixty miles, and

Heber, Utah, one hundred and twenty-five miles. Green River, Wyoming, and Provo, Utah, each one hundred and sixty miles, were the nearest accessible railroad and telegraph stations, and Fort Douglass, at Salt Lake City, two hundred miles, the nearest army post.

The Reservation consists mostly of mountains and deserts. On Green, DuChesne and White Rivers, and a few smaller streams, there are some irrigable valleys, which, with water, could be made highly productive. But of the two million acres embraced in its limits not one could be relied on to produce a crop of any kind without irrigation.

It is almost a rainless region. On the mountain ranges there is a great deal of snow in the winter, but at the Agency it is not unusual to see three hundred and fifty perfectly clear days in the year. Indeed, the Reservation has been described as so many "acres of clear sky."

Soon after I had installed myself as Acting Agent, the employes all came in together to report.

At the head of the roll was Mr. W. A. McKewen, the clerk, whom I afterwards came to know as one of the most capable and trustworthy clerks in the service, and as brave a young man as ever ventured into Indian country. He was a native of Baltimore, and only twenty-three years old. His business education was of the most excellent character, and no matter what his associations or surroundings were, he always demeaned himself as a well-bred, honorable and manly young man.

W. A. McKewen.

Dr. C. M. Sawtelle, of California, was physician; Stephen A. Dole, nephew of a former Commissioner of Indian Affairs, was commissary clerk; John Blankenship, the only one who had a family, was farmer; E. W. Davis was carpenter; Bertram Haight blacksmith; John McAndrews chief herder, and John A. McDonald and Frank Gidney herders. No Agent ever had a better force, in proportion to numbers. They were well suited to their respective places, and were always cheerful, obedient and faithful in the performance of every duty.

On the second day we began the work of making an inventory of the Agency property. The Agents are charged with all property sent to their Agencies, and are required to make quarterly settlements, in which they take credit for everything issued to the Indians, or lost, destroyed, or expended in the service.

The annual supplies are furnished upon contracts which are extensively advertised for and publicly let in

New York and San Francisco by the Commissioner of Indian Affairs upon estimates submitted by the Agents. These supplies consist of beef, flour, salt, bacon, sugar, coffee, beans, soap, blankets, shawls, shoes, clothing, wagons, farm implements, Agency equipments, school and medical supplies. The beef is always delivered on foot at the Agencies by the contractors themselves, but all the other supplies are generally transported from the principal markets of the country by transportation contractors. Sometimes in emergencies Agents are furnished with money and authorized to purchase certain supplies themselves in open market in the vicinity of their Agencies.

One item of the public property for which the Agent at Ouray was responsible was a herd of two thousand five hundred head of cattle, scattered over a meagre, sagebrush range fifty miles in extent. Another at Uintah Agency was "one irrigating canal, nine miles long," and it was the only piece of Government property that I ever receipted for with a feeling of safety.

Before the close of the first day news of my arrival had been carried by runners to all parts of the Reservation—even to Colorow's band in Colorado—and in the afternoon a runner came from Saponero to ask when I was going up to his camp to hold a council with him and his people. He was then camped six or seven miles up DuChesne River.

Manifestly this was a play of the wily old savage to test my executive strength and skill. I told the runner to go back and tell him that for some days I would be occupied with business at the Agency, but that if *any* Indian on the Reservation *had anything to say to me* I would hear him *at the office* whenever it suited him to come.

After hanging about the office and watching me two or three hours, with his blanket drawn up so as to conceal all of his face except just one eye, the runner suddenly turned from the doorcasing where he had been peeping in, mounted his pony and started back to camp in a lope, the usual gait of the blanket Indian on horseback.

Late in the afternoon two young head men came down and told me that Colorow was expected to arrive that night, and that he and Saponero and all the under chiefs and head men of the tribe would come in on the following day to hold a long council with me on business of the greatest importance.

A council called for by the Indians themselves was exactly what I wanted. I had confidence enough in myself to believe that if I could get them to talking with me I could pacify them, at least temporarily, and avert an outbreak. Indeed, that seemed to be our only hope. And to carry out that plan I knew I would have to hold on firmly to my authority as Agent, show no uneasiness, and perhaps make free use of the strategem known in the vernacular of the West as "bluff."

About 9 o'clock next morning, as Mr. McKewen and I were crossing the plaza to the office, we saw a brilliantly costumed and splendidly mounted Indian ascend from DuChesne River bottom about a mile away, on the road leading down from Uintah Agency. He sat his horse like a knight of old, and as the rays of the morning sun flashed on the tinsel of his costume he was as magnificent a figure as I ever saw on horseback. It was Saponero.

As we stood and looked another Indian came in sight, about five paces behind the first, and then another about the same distance in rear of the second, and in that order they continued to come until we had counted one hundred and forty-two. From that point the road ran half a mile at an oblique angle, and as they stretched away in single file, and marched in a slow walk, broadside to us, across the level mesa, they presented a truly imposing savage array.

Colorow, accompanied by twenty-five or thirty men, but no women or children, had come in very early in the morning and established camp near the Agency. They looked like they had traveled all night, and we afterwards found out that they had in fact come from

Garfield County, Colorado, fifty or sixty miles distant, since sunset the evening before.

Saponero and his followers rode straight to Colorow's camp, where about three-fourths of them immediately dismounted and seated themselves flat on the ground for a council with the Colorado band, leaving the rest holding the horses.

CHAPTER XIII.

MY FIRST COUNCIL WITH THE UTES—SAPONERO, COL-
OROW AND CAPTAIN BILLY—"A PURTY GOOD IDEA"
—EXTRICATED FROM A DANGEROUS DILEMMA BY A
YOUNG SQUAW INTERPRETER.

THE council at Colorow's camp lasted about an
hour. At its conclusion the Indians all came
across the plaza to the office, Saponero and Colorow
walking together in front. As many as could find
room in the large office crowded in and seated themselves on the floor, and all the rest bunched up against
the door and windows, the pony holders crowding close
upon the heels of those standing on the ground.

A good natured, happy sort of an Indian named
Captain Billy had previously been introduced to me as
the Agency interpreter. He was now seated flat on
the floor at the right-hand of Saponero, whom he evidently regarded as the greatest man on earth, and the
comical, owl-like expression of his countenance showed
that he was almost overwhelmed by his sense of the
gravity of the occasion and the tremendous responsibili-
ties of his position.

And ominous as the situation seemed to be, I could not refrain from laughing outright when I turned from Captain Billy to take a good look at Colorow and thought about Bill Nye's humorous biographical sketch of him as Brigadier General Wm. H. Colorow. Colorow's wardrobe had probably never contained anything more military than paint and feathers, and nothing could have been more ridiculous than the thought of that stalwart old "coffee cooler" strutting around in striped trousers, plumed hat, shoulder straps, sash and sabre, unless it was the figure which he himself cut at the Denver Exposition the year before. On that occasion he fell into the hands of some mischievous drummers who dressed him up in one of their beautifully embroidered night robes and turned him loose in the exposition hall in broad daylight in that usually secluded garment. The old man was entirely guileless, and innocently and proudly paraded the streets and exposition hall in his "white man coat," as he called it, until the police enticed him into a patrol wagon and hauled him off to the guardhouse, where they double-teamed on him and made him swap his beautiful robe of many frills and figures for a dingy old horse blanket.

When all the Indians had settled themselves on the floor and become quiet, Saponero slowly arose, advanced and shook hands with me, and, with great solemnity, began his speech.

Saponero was of medium height, lean and sinewy, and apparently sixty years of age.   Hard lines marked all of his features.   One could almost doubt that they had ever been illuminated by a more genial light than the smile of incredulity and derision.   Evidences of strong individuality, obstinacy, savage ignorance and superstition were visible in his face, but the things plainest to be seen in the gleam of his eyes and the curl and quiver of his lips were hatred of the white race, and a heart troubled to the point of absolute desperation.

Beginning slowly, he spoke a few sentences with remarkable ease and dignity, and then paused for Captain Billy to interpret his words to me in English, which, to my astonishment, the Captain proceeded to do as follows:

"Saponero say he glad to see you.   All lee Injuns glad to see you.   Maybe Washington send you to tend to it some business for Injun.   Maybe dat purty good idea."

"What else did he say?" I asked, "that is not all."

"Dat's all Saponero say," he replied, as he nodded with great assurance to the chief to go ahead.   At the next pause, instead of attempting to interpret that part, he coolly waved it aside as if it was of no consequence whatever, and merely said by way of explanation:

"Oh, Saponero, maybe he jes talk about it some tings long time ago.   Dat make no diffunce."

"Look here, now," I commanded, "no more 'maybe so' and 'dat make no diffunce.' You tell me what Saponero says."

"Yes. I telly you what Saponero say. Dat's de bes' way," he replied.

Saponero's next sentence was a long one. When he paused Billy said:

"Saponero he talk about it long time ago make it de treaty. I speck he want to talk about it white man shoot at Colorow, and steal Injun Reservation, annuity money, everything, and Injun heap mad now and purty soon fight. I speck Saponero want to talk about it heap o' tings like dat. Dat purty good idea."

"Yes, I 'speck' so myself; but why don't you tell me what he does say?" I demanded rather sharply.

"Dat's all Saponero say—jes like I tell you," he answered.

By this time I was satisfied that the Captain was an interpreter who could not interpret—who could not speak English much better than I could speak Ute. I asked Mr. McKewen if we could not get a more capable person. He said that there was but one other Indian on the Reservation who could interpret even as well as Captain Billy, and that was a squaw. She was then living with relatives in camp near the Agency, but she had been reared in a Mormon family, and was a great deal more competent than the Captain.   We sent for her.

Saponero then delivered another section of his speech, and when he paused that time Captain Billy said:

"Jes like I tell you.   Saponero jes talk about it some tings long time ago.   Maybe some tings about treaty. Maybe Washington tell you about it dat treaty.   Dat purty good idea.   Long time ago Uncompahgres live in Colorado.   By and by make it dat treaty and come over dis side line.   Now, fust ting Injun know white man steal it de line.   Maybe dat what Saponero talk about."

"Maybe so, you pop-eyed bronco!   Don't you *know* what he is talking about?" I said with some severity, for I realized the great danger of trying to hold a council with Indians, especially in their then desperate frame of mind, through an ignorant interpreter.   He replied:

"Saponero talk about treaty—jes like I tell you. Dat treaty purty good idea, Saponero say."

Manifestly it was not only useless, but positively dangerous, to continue the council with him.   He seemed to be doing the best he could, but his mental vision was so narrow and his knowledge of the English language so nearly limited to the phrase "purty good idea," that, however good his intentions, he was liable to convey erroneous impressions to the minds of the Indians, or lead them into positive misunderstandings, that, instead of allaying their dissatisfaction, might increase it even to the point of precipitating trouble at once.

Seeing no other "purty good idea" leading out of this dilemma, I frankly told Captain Billy that his English was but little more intelligible to me than undiluted Ute—that in fact I was not sure that I could understand him any better than I could Saponero—and asked him to tell Saponero that I had sent for the girl to help interpret, and thought it safer to await her arrival. How he interpreted it to Saponero of course the Indians and the Great Spirit alone know. But whether he did it correctly or incorrectly, it greatly intensified the look of distress in the old man's already painfully troubled face.

Saponero turned to Colorow and conversed with him and the other chiefs in a very earnest and much troubled manner for five or ten minutes. Then Colorow arose, shook hands with me, and proceeded to speak, his voice unmistakably betraying suppressed anger and excitement.

Captain Billy's face had assumed a look of bewilderment, and I was satisfied that he had blundered badly in his interpretation of my words and meaning to the Indians. Because of this, and the actions of Colorow, Saponero and several others, I began to fear that they might become aroused to action before the girl interpreter could come to our rescue.

When Colorow had spoken several sentences, he motioned to Captain Billy, who said:

"Colorow say all lee Injuns' hearts heap sick. Bad white mans make it a heap o' troubles. Maybe some Injuns purty quick fight now. Young men heap mad —heap bad talk. Squaws jes all time cry. Colorow say hole on little bit, maybe Washington fix it. Young men say 'No; Washington heap talk—jes all time talk —but no fix it.' Purty bad. Colorado cattlemans shoot at Colorow, maybe so seventeen times, maybe so forty times, yudder day. Shoot two Colorow's young men, and kill it Colorow's pony. What you tink of it dat, Colorow say?"

Of course! What *did* I think of it, that? Evidently Colorow was magnanimous enough to allow the "Colorado cattlemans" to state their side of the case themselves, for he refrained from any allusion to the fact that he and his band had shot back at them perhaps three or four times "seventeen or forty times," and chased them clear out of Garfield County. I told McKewen in undertone that I intended to evade the question if I could, but if pressed for an answer I believed I should frankly admit to the old man that as matters then stood I was very much dissatisfied with the marksmanship of the "Colorado cattlemans," and asked him what he thought about it, as he seemed to be doing considerable thinking just then. He replied that "a band of men who had opportunity to shoot seventeen or forty times at Colorow and failed to kill him deserved to be driven out of the *State*."

Just then the messenger came in with the young squaw interpreter. Declining a chair which I offered her, she sat down on the floor by the side of Captain Billy. I told her why I had sent for her, and asked her to explain it to the Indians, which she did. From the time that Captain Billy told them that I had sent for her they had been doing a great deal of talking among themselves, and her statement set half of them to talking and grunting at once, which seemed to startle her. Finally Saponero arose, waved his hand over the crowd, said something which produced silence, and then turning to me, began to speak. I saw the girl cower. When he paused and motioned to her, she said, in a clear voice and distinct articulation:

"Saponero tells me to tell you that I am a squaw, and that Ute chiefs and warriors do not sit in council with squaws; that I must keep my lips closed; that Billy is the interpreter, and he must interpret."

Turning again to McKewen, whose exasperation and sense of danger was about to overcome his usual patience and amiability, I asked him what he would think of a cattleman, or any other sort of man, who could not hit

Saponero the first fire?   For answer he said he wished he had a big cannon loaded with buckshot and tacks with which to take what a hunter would call "a pot shot" at the whole crowd.

All efforts to induce Saponero to allow the girl to interpret proving futile, and determining to take no further risk with Captain Billy, I had made up my mind to give up the council as a failure when the girl volunteered the information that a competent white interpreter named James Davis was then visiting his brother, an employe at Uintah, and she had no doubt he would come to our assistance if requested to do so.

Saponero being acquainted with Davis, he readily assented to an adjournment of the council until I could send for him, and as this was announced every Indian present mounted his pony and departed for camp in a lope, not one waiting for another, and the chiefs barely taking time to shake hands with me and McKewen as they hurried out of the office.

CHAPTER XIV.

ORDERED TO UINTAH AGENCY — TAKE CHARGE OF
THAT AGENCY ALSO — THE UINTAH AND WHITE
RIVER UTES — DESCRIPTION OF THE RESERVATION
AND AGENCY.

ON the second day after the council described in
the preceding chapter, I received a dispatch to
proceed immediately to Uintah and take charge of that
Agency also.

It is hardly necessary to say that I could not regard
this order otherwise than as the reverse of what Captain
Billy would call "a purty good idea " It threw the re-
sponsibilities of both Agencies upon me at a most critical time and subjected mc and the employes to the
great hardship and danger of frequent trips between the
two places. It also conveyed the information that the
two Agencies were to be consolidated, and that there-
after all the Indians on both Reservations were to be
under one Agent—*or one Agent under all the Indians*,
as the scales might finally turn—information which, in
the very nature of the case, it would be impossible to

long conceal from them, and which McKewen and I knew would greatly augment the dissatisfaction of the Uncompahgres, at least, and perhaps blot out any good impression or pacificatory effect that our recent council may have had upon them.

But right or wrong, prudent or ill-considered, the order had to be obeyed, and leaving McKewen as my representative at Ouray, I started to Uintah at sunrise the next morning, accompanied by Mr. Davis, the Ouray carpenter.

Seven miles out from the Agency we left the main road on the mesa and drove down into DuChesne bottom to pay our respects to Saponero, who was encamped there with his entire individual band, which Davis said consisted of about six hundred Indians and two thousand dogs. The old man was glad to see us, and as he disliked the Agent at Uintah, he was also pleased to hear that he had been "cut off," as the Indians call a dismissal.

We arrived at Uintah at 4 o'clock in the afternoon. As we drove up we saw a man in shirt sleeves standing in front of one of the traders' stores, whom I instinctively recognized as the Agent. He was looking at us with his hat cocked over on one side of his head and his thumbs hitched in the arm holes of his vest. The thought flashed through my mind that certainly the

Indians could hardly be blamed for merely kicking him, as they were reported to have recently done.

Standing in the office door was a pug-nosed young man whom I recognized in like manner as the clerk. His hair had just been mowed down to the skin with barbers' clippers, prison style, and as he stood there in high heeled boots, red flannel shirt and corduroy trousers, holding a broad-brimmed white hat in his hand, and with a countenance to match, I wondered why the Indians had not kicked him some too.

The Agent having been notified from Washington to be ready for me, he requested me to relieve him at once, which I did, and immediately dismissed the clerk also.

As may be imagined, my sudden arrival and assumption of authority, and summary dismissal of the clerk, produced something of a panic among the employes.   From the office I could see them dodging about as if each one expected his time to come next.

The Indians belonging to Uintah Agency are the Uintah and White River Bands of Utes—the former numbering 500 and the latter 600.   The Uintahs are by far the most tractable and peaceably disposed of all the Utes, but it can hardly be said that they are any more enlightened than the rest of the tribe.

And the White Rivers have even a worse reputation and more bloody history than the Uncompahgres. They are the identical Indians who, less than seven years before, or in September, 1879, committed the Meeker Massacre, and fought the battle in which Major Thornburgh was killed.

They then belonged to the White River Agency in Colorado, and Meeker was their Agent. Suddenly one day they broke out and killed and mutilated in the most shockingly barbarous manner every white person on the Reservation, except the Agent's wife and daughter, and the Agency farmer's wife, who escaped death by hiding, but were afterwards discovered and held in horrible captivity for three months.

It is said that the chiefs themselves killed the Agent as they were returning with him to the office from his house, where they had just been his guests at dinner, and that the massacre was all over with in thirty minutes.

A few days later they attacked a column of troops under Major Thornburgh, as it was marching through a canyon to the relief of the Agency. The attack lasted two days, and the troops suffered terribly in killed and wounded, Major Thornburgh himself being killed at the first fire. The Indians were so securely concealed and intrenched behind the rocks on the walls of the canyon that the troops could neither see them nor dislodge them, and every time a soldier exposed himself to their sight he was instantly killed or wounded.   The entire command was held in this critical situation until re-enforcements arrived and came down on the Indians from above.

Their punishment for that outbreak had been extremely light, and now they were reported to be again discontented and threatening.

The Uintah Reservation, which is occupied in common by the White Rivers and the Uintahs, embraces the famous valley of the DuChesne River and its tributaries — the Strawberry and Uintah Rivers, and many smaller streams.

This is the finest valley in Utah, the justly renowned valley of the Great Salt Lake not excepted.   Its length is estimated at eighty miles, and its average width at twenty-five miles.   It is abundantly watered, and nearly all irrigable.   The surface is generally smooth, though with enough slope to give good velocity to all the water courses, which, being mostly fed by melting snows in the mountains, are fuller in summer than in winter.

Notwithstanding it has a mean elevation of perhaps six thousand feet above the sea, the valley has the form of a basin, being entirely encircled by the Uintah Mountains.   The atmosphere is so wonderfully clear that this lofty mountain wall may be plainly seen entirely across from one end or one side of the valley to the other. Coming down the valley on the road from Salt Lake City the Agency office—only one story high—can be seen a distance of forty miles. From the office door I have seen covered wagons a distance of twelve miles, and with a spyglass I have seen horses up at the snow-line on Mount Gilbert, which I was told was fifteen miles. Mount Gilbert is the highest peak in Utah, and is perpetually snow-capped. It sits directly in the rear, and in plain view, of the Agency.

The Agency is located at White Rocks post office, near Uintah River. The buildings consist of Agency office and warehouse, council house, saw and grist mill, blacksmith shop, wood shop, barn, doctor's office, schoolhouse, Agent's dwelling, several employes' dwellings, and two traders' stores and dwellings. These buildings all front on a plaza about seventy-five yards wide and a hundred and fifty yards long. The elevation of the place is said to be six thousand six hundred feet above sea level, and rains are almost as infrequent there as at Ouray.

CHAPTER XV.

THE EMPLOYES AT UINTAH—OMINOUS MOVEMENTS—
WHITE MEN INSTIGATING THE INDIANS TO AN OUT-
BREAK—A CLUE TO THE PLOT.

EARLY next morning I summoned all the employes to the office. As they filed in uneasiness was plainly depicted in all their faces, and some of them even looked as if they expected something awful to happen. Dr. B. D. Williams was physician, John Hemsworth farmer, Abraham Coon carpenter, Enoch Davis blacksmith, Frank Boan and Clarence A. Granger herders. They had all been appointed from Utah, except Dr. Williams, who was from Alabama, and Mr. Hemsworth, who was from Missouri.

After receiving reports from them concerning their respective departments, I said a few words to them which produced a remarkable change in their countenances, and they returned to their work expressing great satisfaction with the "council," as they called it.

The remainder of the forenoon was devoted to looking over the Agency and getting acquainted with its equipments. In the afternoon we began making an inventory of the property, and were occupied at that work most of the time during the next ten days.

Very little had been seen of the White Rivers since my arrival, and by the time we had completed the inventory they had ceased their visits to the office almost entirely, and were reported to be spending nearly all their time in council at Chief Sowawick's camp, which was situated only a little over a mile from the Agency, but in a secluded place on the opposite side of White Rocks Creek.

These signs, and increasing indications of restlessness and discontent among some of the young bucks of the Uintah band, were beginning to be regarded by the employes and myself as ominous of danger, and I was in the act of sending for the White River chiefs to come in and explain their meaning when Big Tom, Antero, Tokawana and two or three other Uintah chiefs, voluntarily appeared at the office and gave me that information themselves.

In the few previous interviews that I had had with these Uintahs I had listened to them with patience and sympathy, as I always tried to do with all Indians, and I now had the satisfaction of seeing them disposed to talk with me in unreserved confidence.

Big Tom's speech embraced all that was said by

UINTAH AGENCY, UTAH.

them all, and was interpreted to me in substance as follows:

"Big Tom hears a heap of bad talk. He comes to ask you what it means. White men come among us and tell us that soldiers are coming pretty soon to make trouble. Every day for more than one moon white men have been telling this to our young men on the border, and now they are coming among our camps and telling it to our chiefs, and even to our squaws and pappooses."

"We Uintah chiefs have paid no attention to this talk. We knew that no wrong had been done by any of our band, and we have had brave hearts. We have felt no fear that our Great Father would suffer his soldiers to hurt any of us; we are his children. We have always walked in the road that he and our little fathers (Agents) have pointed out to us, as well as we could. But we ask him to remember that it is a new road to us. There are many things which we do not know how to do like our white brother. It will take us a long time to learn. But we have always lived at peace with our palefaced neighbors. Go into our wickiups and you will find no white scalps. There is no blood on our hands. We love peace. It makes our hearts glad to see our squaws and pappooses laugh and play and sleep sound."

"But sometimes our young men listen to bad talk—

maybe bad white men—and want to go a crooked road. That gives us a great deal of trouble.   We have to be patient.   Our Great Father should remember all these things and forbear with us as we have to forbear with our children.''

"But two sleeps ago two white men came to Sowa-wick's camp in the dark and told him that the big soldier chief, General Crook, was coming with a big band of soldiers, to kill some of the Uncompahgre, White River and Uintah chiefs, and put the others in the big guardhouse (penitentiary) and take all the rest of the tribe away off somewhere and give our Res-ervation to the white man.   They said the soldiers would be here in ten sleeps; that they saw them getting off the cars at Evanston themselves, and talked with them. These white men said they were our friends, and had hurried back to tell us.   They said we ought to go and drive off all the white people, and take all the beef and flour, and everything else, at Uintah and Ouray, and then go and meet the soldiers in the canyons and fight them.   Two other white men went on to Saponero's camp and told him the same thing.''

"The young men of the Uncompahgre and White River Bands are heap mad.   Heap bad talk—talk about fight.   The chiefs counseled peace until last night. Last night they gave their consent, and now their squaws and pappooses are running to the mountains, and the warriors are getting ready to fight. Maybe so fight to-day, maybe so to-morrow. Don't know.''

"It is mighty bad. Many of *our* young men are breaking away from us and going over to the Uncompahgres and White Rivers to help them fight. Maybe so some of them love Uncompahgre and White River squaws. Maybe so some of them just hot-headed and foolish. But they ask us why Washington soldiers are coming to kill our chiefs and take us all away off somewhere and give our Reservation to the white man. We cannot answer. We do not know. They go. We cannot stop them.''

"Our chief, Tabbe, is a very old man. He is weak, and blind and falls down just like a little pappoose. But Tabbe is a good man—*good* man. He has always kept his young men in the Great Father's road, and lived in peace with the white man. Now the Great Father sends his soldiers to kill Tabbe—*good* man—*old* man—and drive all his people from their homes away off somewhere, they know not where. Tabbe's heart heap sick. Last night Big Tom see him, Tabbe. Tabbe say, 'you go and ask him, the Agent, what's the matter.' We come to ask you about it.''

"It is mighty bad, mighty bad. We want peace. But we cannot stand still and let the soldiers come and kill us. Life is sweet to us as it is to our white brother. We love our squaws and pappooses, and they would rather die than be taken away from this valley. We have lived here all our lives. All the dead of our tribe for generations and generations are buried here. We love the very earth under our feet, the air we breathe, the sun that shines on us, the plains, the mountains, this beautiful valley, and the clear running waters. We know no other country. We could never love any other as well.''

''But our squaws and pappooses are heap scared. They catch hold of us and tremble, and at night they are afraid to go to sleep. They just all the time cry and look for it the soldiers. Our hearts are heap sick. Two suns have come and gone since we closed our eyes in sleep.''

''This is Big Tom's talk. What you say? I ask you now?''

I hope it is needless for me to say that I was deeply touched. I had heard nearly all the employes speak of Big Tom as a good Indian. He was the confidential friend and personal representative of the blind and decrepit old chief, Tabbe, who was held in high respect by the employes because of his peaceable disposition towards the whites during the many years that he had been the active and advisory leader of his band. I had no doubt of the sincerity of his wish to avert trouble for peace sake alone.   Moreover, his speech had confirmed my suspicions that the Indians were being instigated to an outbreak by white men, and although he did not know their names, or where they lived, his language left no room for doubt in my mind as to their general identity, or their motives.

"Hurried back from Evanston to tell their friends, the Indians, that troops were coming to kill and imprison their chiefs, and take all the rest away off somewhere and give their Reservation to the white man.   Ought to sack both Agencies and meet the troops in the canyons and fight them."

What did those statements imply?   What better clue to the plot could be desired than they contained?

I pitied Big Tom and his people sincerely, but the strongest emotion I felt was hot indignation at the heartlessness of the scheme by which it was now clear to me that they were about to be deluded to their own destruction, for the circumstance must not be overlooked that it not only involved the lives and fortunes of the Indians, but it also placed the lives of all the people at both Agencies, including my own, in jeopardy.

And with my rising indignation all my sensations of fear gave way to an eagerness to expose the plot to the whole tribe, and a strong feeling of confidence in my ability to stay the uplifted hand, and turn the attempted mischief to good account in pacifying the Indians, if I could only get the White Rivers into council and word to the Uncompahgres before a blow was struck.

But from Big Tom's statement the Uncompahgres and White Rivers were both ready, and liable to begin at any moment, as the latter had done at Meeker less than seven years before. It was now near nightfall and a council could not be had with the White Rivers, or word communicated to the Uncompahgres until next morning.

And what could I say or do to hold the situation in *statu quo* until that time? What would it be discreet to say to Big Tom? It would not do to turn him away with a palpable evasion. And yet the most insignificant imprudent utterance, or the most prudent statement slightly misunderstood, might precipitate an attack at once.

I could not tell him that the troops were not coming, because, even if they had not been seen at Evanston, I had been advised that they *would* come soon. And if they *were* coming, was not that confirmatory of all that the Indians had been told by their night riding white "friends?"

But my mind was made up by the time Big Tom had ceased speaking. There was but one thing to do, and
(5)

I determined to do it with energy and boldness. I congratulated him and his colleagues earnestly upon their good sense and obedience in coming to talk with me, instead of doing as the White River chiefs were doing.

I told them also that I desired to have a council with all the Uintahs and White Rivers at the Agency at 8 o'clock next morning, to tell them the truth about what they had heard, and show them how they were about to be led into an awful mistake, and asked them if they would all go immediately to Sowawick's camp and tell him I wanted him and his people to come, and bring back word to me whether they would or not. I also asked them to send a runner through to Saponero that night to ask him and his people to meet me at Ouray for a council on the day after the morrow. Instead of hesitating, they seemed glad to comply with my requests, and departed at once for Sowawick's camp.

Immediately after the Meeker Massacre the Department had caused forty Springfield rifles and ten thousand cartridges to be sent to the Agency for use in emergency. They had never been unboxed. I distributed them among the employes, and made all other necessary preparations for defense. There were about twenty guns and forty pistols at the Agency besides these.

I selected a log house that had a stream of water under it, to use as a sort of fort, and caused some heavy slabs, big spikes and a sledge hammer to be put in, with which to close the doors and windows. I also had some provisions put in, and some picks, spades, shovels and axes. My idea was that by firing other buildings the Indians might run us out, and in that case it was my plan to get out on the level ground, where they would have no cover for approach, and throw up a little fort. And thinking of just such an emergency as this, I had only a day or two before caused four saw logs to be casually dropped almost in a square, right where I thought the fort ought to be. With another log all around on top of these to protect our heads, with notches cut in the bottom for port holes, we would have a good fort without any digging, except for water, which was obtainable anywhere there at a depth of five or six feet.

Shortly after dark Big Tom and his crowd returned to tell me that the White Rivers were all ready to fight, but had promised to hold up and come and hear what I had to say.

I detailed two of the employes to stand watch in the first part of the night, and two in the latter part. Indians rode about the Agency all night long with their ponies' feet muffled so that they made no more noise than kittens would have done, and we afterwards learned that they had been doing that every night for a week, and also slipping about the houses on foot.

CHAPTER XVI.

A COUNCIL WITH THE INDIANS—THE PLOT UNFOLDED
—THE EFFECT—HENRY JIM STARTS TO OURAY TO
TELL SAPONERO.

AT 8 o'clock next morning the Indians came in to
the council.

The Uintah chiefs looked even more careworn and
anxious than they did the evening before. Many of
their young men came with the White Rivers, were
heavily armed, and looked black and sullen.

Among the White Rivers pistols could be seen protruding from the folds of nearly every blanket. Every
belt was full of cartridges, and a Winchester rifle was
slung to every saddle. Sowawick, the principal chief,
had two large revolvers buckled on outside of his
blanket. They left all their ponies standing in a bunch,
and quite a large number of bucks remained with them
and did not come in to the council house at all—a most
unusual circumstance.

I had cautioned the employes to stay within easy

reach of their arms, and to appear to be at their custo-
mary duties, as if nothing unusual was taking place.

James Davis happened to be at the Agency with his
brother, the blacksmith, and he willingly agreed to go
into the council with me as interpreter, as I was afraid
to trust entirely to Charlie Mack, the Indian interpreter.

Instructions were given for no other white person to
come about the council.   I wanted the Indians to see
that Davis and I were not afraid to go in alone.

Davis had one good pistol, and I gave him two more,
and filled his pockets full of cartridges.   I also put two
revolvers in my own pockets and buckled two around me.

I had caused about twenty chairs to be taken into the
council house and placed in rows facing two that I had
set against the rear wall for Davis and myself.   When
the Indians came in I made Big Tom and Sowawick sit
down side by side directly in front of me.   In fact I
assumed the duties of an usher, picked out an Indian
for each chair, and seated the entire crowd just as I
wanted them to sit.

I did this partly for our advantage in case of an outbreak, but mainly to avert such an occurrence by mysti-
fying and intimidating the Indians, and giving them to
understand that I intended that mine should be the
guiding hand.   I saw in a minute that it was good
tactics, and had produced exactly the look of bewilderment and hesitancy that I had calculated on.

Believing that it would also have a subduing effect on the Indians to know how Davis and I were armed, I picked a chance and slipped the two pistols out of my pockets and tucked them under my belt in front of those in the scabbards, where they could be seen, and yet not appear to be purposely displayed.

When all got quiet I rapped the council to order and spoke as follows:

"I speak to the Uintahs and White Rivers. I sent word to you that I had some important news to tell you. It will save you a great deal of trouble if you listen to it. Some bad white men who live here close around your Reservation want to take it from you. They are trying to get you into a fight with Washington so that they can then come in and take your country. That is what I want to tell you about."

"I am glad to see that Big Tom and the rest of the Uintah chiefs have come in unarmed and friendly, and appear to want to listen like sensible men. That is the way for men to do who want to do right."

"But I notice that all the White Rivers have guns and pistols, and look mad and ugly. Sowawick himself has two pistols buckled around him, and his face is as black as midnight."

"Washington has sent me among a great many different tribes, but I never thought it necessary to carry weapons until I saw the White Rivers ride up here this morning just like a war party.   Then I told all the white people to stay close by their guns outside; and when I saw that Sowawick had left fifty of his young men to guard his ponies, and was coming in here with those two pistols buckled around him—when I saw all that I say—I armed myself with these four pistols, two for my right hand and two for my left hand."

"If you will listen to me your country will not be taken from you.   Washington does not want to take it.   But these bad white men are trying to get it.   If you want me to tell you all about it I will do it.   You ought to know it.   But the White Rivers look as if they had come to fight, and not to listen.   If their ears are closed against the truth I will not talk.   If they have come to fight, I want them to begin now while we are all in here together, because Davis and I are ready, and so are the white people outside."

All this was pure bluff, of course; especially the reference to two pistols for each hand, for I had never fired a pistol with my left hand in my life, and was a poor shot with my right hand.

My purpose was to show the Uintahs that the White Rivers were blind and reckless; that their decision to fight was without excuse and against the best interests of all the tribe; that it might result in losing their country instead of saving it; that their pretended white friends were instigating them to their own destruction; to force the White Rivers themselves to acknowledge all this and offer some atonement for it. It was my aim to allude to these things in such way as to make the desire of both bands to hear more irresistible, because I was satisfied that the White Rivers had come to denounce and threaten as well as to listen, and to listen only with incredulous ears.

And I am satisfied that it was our salvation. It was evident that Sowawick had anticipated nothing of the kind, and was disconcerted. He arose and started to explain and make excuses. But it was my intention to suffer no one to speak until I had prepared the ground and sown all the seed that I wanted to sow. I told him to wait; to listen to me, and when I got through I would listen to him. Then I continued as follows:

"I speak to Big Tom, to Sowawick and to all their people. Listen to what I say. You have a good country—the loveliest valley in Utah. Beautiful running waters—cold and good in the hot summer time from the melting snows in the mountains; rich grass in the valleys for your ponies; deer and elk in the mountains for meat and buckskin; mountains all around to shelter you from cold winds in the winter."

"Washington knows that you love this country, and

he wants you to keep it. He has no thought of taking it away from you. But he requires that you shall do right. You must stay on your Reservation and do no wrong to one another or any white person on the outside.''

''Washington has heard of a great deal of bad talk, and of some bad things that have been done. You know what they are. It is unnecessary for me to name them. Maybe bad Indians; maybe bad white man; maybe both do wrong. Washington does not like that. He is sending his soldiers to stop it. They are coming now from Evanston. Will be here in four or five sleeps. They will sit down somewhere on the Reservation and live here all the time. If any white man intrudes upon the Reservation I will tell them and they will throw him out. If Sowawick or any other Indian hurts anybody I will tell them about that and they will catch *him* and put *him* in the guardhouse. To make it plain they are coming to catch both whites and Indians when they do wrong, but they will make no trouble for those who do right.''

''White men have told you that Washington is sending these soldiers to take your country away from you and give it to the white man. That is not the truth. The men who tell you that want your country themselves. They see but one way to get it, and that is to blind your eyes with talk, and get you to sack the Agencies or fight the soldiers, or do some other great wrong, that would cause Washington to take your country away from you and drive you off somewhere else as punishment.   Then these men being right here on the line they could come in and take this beautiful valley of yours before the white men who live a long way off could get here.   You think these men are your friends. I have no doubt they are in a great many things.   But they covet your Reservation.   You can see as well as I that all other valleys in Utah are full of white people. They need more land that they can cultivate.   Your large and beautiful valley would furnish homes for thousands of them.   They want it badly, and if you rush blindly into war with Washington they may get it.   I do not know.''

''But the chiefs ought to think about all these things before they fight.   They will lose everything and gain nothing.   If you go on the warpath Washington will send enough soldiers here to drive you out of this valley.   Then where will the Utes go?   What will become of their squaws and pappooses?   Look to the north, to the south, to the east, to the west, look everywhere, and you see white men.''

''Suppose you go to the mountains.   The soldiers will swarm after you and catch you there.   Geronimo

—Apache chief—you know him.   Where is Geronimo now?   He went on the warpath.   Too many soldiers came.   Geronimo fled to the mountains.   The soldiers followed.   Everywhere Geronimo went the soldiers were before him—behind him—all around him—heap of soldiers.   The other day they caught him.   They have carried him to St. Augustine, Florida, away down by the big water, Atlantic Ocean.   Apaches no more see him, Geronimo.   Maybe so mosquitoes eat him up, maybe so alligators catch him, maybe so Washington drop a pile driver on him.   Don't know.''

''The time may have been in the past when you could hold your own on the warpath, but it now leads to swift and sure destruction.   To take it to-day is to seal the doom of all your squaws and pappooses.   Follow the Washington road and you will hold your country and enjoy peace and happiness.''

''Now go back to your homes, bring your squaws and pappooses back from the mountains, carry your guns and pistols only when you go to kill game, and stop being foolish.   If any of those white men come on the Reservation again, bring them to me and I will put them in the guardhouse.   Go about your own business like sensible men, do no harm to anybody, and if anything goes wrong with you, or you hear any bad talk, come and tell me about it.   When I need help to keep down trouble, come and help me.   This is my talk.''

It was worth an admission fee to see the expressions on their faces and hear their grunts when the interpreter explained what I said about the mosquitoes, alligators and pile driver, in connection with Geronimo's fate. And altogether the effect of the speech was extraordinary —quite beyond my expectations.

Big Tom and Henry Jim—the latter an Uncompahgre chief who happened to be present—were in raptures and eager to speak; but to carry out my plan to the end, I told them to let Sowawick speak first.

Sowawick was completely upset. He arose with palpable embarrassment. It was evident that he did not know how to begin, or what to say. He spoke slowly, and at first reflected long between sentences. He said:

"It is true that my people have been very much excited and alarmed, but you ought not to judge us harshly. In your mind put yourself in our places. Men whom we supposed were our friends told us that the soldiers were coming to kill our chiefs, and drive our people away off somewhere and give our country to the white man, and we believed it. We could not see what else the soldiers were coming for. Now you tell us differently and we are glad to hear it. Your talk is good, and we feel secure. We would have told you about all this bad talk, but those white men told us not to do that. They said that you and the soldiers were good friends and would act together. We want you to be our friend, and we will tell you all the bad talk we hear and help you keep down trouble. We will not talk about fight anymore without first telling you what is the matter. If the soldiers want to sit down on the Reservation, all right—just so they do not try to hurt us without cause or take our country away from us.''

''The Uncompahgres are scared and getting ready to fight, just as we were doing. You go quick and tell Saponero what you have told us. I will send some of my young men on fast horses to tell him you are coming. His son—young chief—Henry Jim, has heard your talk and says it is good. He will ride fast and tell Saponero. Saponero's heart will feel good.''

Big Tom said:

''Your talk is good—*good* talk. Big Tom's heart is glad. All the Uintah chiefs feel glad. Big Tom will tell Tabbe. Tabbe will be heap glad. Tabbe is good man. Never go crazy, Tabbe. Some Uintah young men act foolish and talk fight. Big Tom will tell them to hold on, stop, be still, do as Agent tells you. If anybody hurts Indian, come and tell Agent. You be our friend. We will help you keep down trouble. We will tell you all the bad talk we hear. We will tell our White River friends to keep still—don't act crazy—you make it a heap of trouble for all of us—make Washing-

ton take our country away from us. That is bad.
White Rivers must not do that. Uintahs will tell you
about that, and help you stop it.''

Henry Jim shook my hand with great earnestness,
and said:

''Henry Jim has heard your talk. He is glad. It is
good talk. Me go now quick to tell Saponero. Saponero heap scared. All Uncompahgre young men heap
scared. All crazy. Want to fight. Me see 'em last
night. Maybe so fight to-day—maybe so to-morrow.
Me go quick and tell Saponero to-day you come. To-
morrow, sun little bit high, you hold it a council at
Ouray. Me tell Saponero hold on—wait—hear Agent
talk—*good* talk. All right. Me go now. My pony
good pony—run fast. To-morrow, daylight, me see you
at Ouray. Good bye.''

He strode rapidly out of the house, followed by five
or six young Uncompahgre bucks. From a window I
saw them mount and start for Ouray in a lope—a gait
which I had no idea would be broken a single time on
the journey—up hill or down—except in fording the
streams.

It was then 12 o'clock and I announced that I would
go to Ouray in the afternoon to hold a council with the
Uncompahgres. The chiefs all said they were glad of
that, and hoped Henry Jim would get there before any-

thing bad had taken place. Sowawick shook hands with me, and pledged me his word that no harm should be done by the Indians in my absence. The council adjourned in perfect good humor, and every white person at the Agency experienced a feeling of happy deliverance, for the time being at least, from imminent peril.

CHAPTER XVII.

THE TRIP TO OURAY—INTENSE EXCITEMENT—THE
INDIANS INTENDED TO ATTACK AT DAYLIGHT—
THE TROOPS HEARD FROM—OBJECTIONS TO THE
"BUFFALO SOLDIERS"—THE TROOPS ARRIVE.

I CARRIED Mr. Davis with me to Ouray. We made
the trip in a buggy, well armed, and with a team of
saddle horses.

Indian lookouts were posted on all the high points
along the road, and many of them intercepted us to
ascertain who we were, and where we were going.

It was an hour after dark when we arrived at Ouray.
Indian runners had apprised the employes of our coming, and they were glad to see us. They had been
momentarily expecting an attack all day. They had
all their horses saddled and bridled, and were standing
watch by turns to guard against surprise.

Saponero and Colorow had sent to the trader's store
at daylight that morning and bought every box of
matches, every foot of rope, every bridle, saddle, cinch
and saddle blanket, every piece of dressed buckskin,

every box of black paint—the war color—and unusually large quantities of various other articles needful on the warpath.

The Indians knew that the trader kept unfixed ammunition—powder, lead and caps.   They called for all he had.   Believing that they would take it away from him if he did not sell it, he sold them some, but succeeded in hiding most of it.

Afterwards one of them found a 15-cent bar of lead and kept increasing his offer for it until it amounted to $4.50, which happened to be all the money he had left, and which, as I recollect, the trader accepted, deeming it unsafe to refuse.

When I arose at daylight next morning, my stalwart friend, Henry Jim, was sitting at my room door, so worn and haggard from fatigue and loss of sleep that I hardly recognized him.

Henry Jim said he arrived at Saponero's camp before night, and found the squaws, old men and pappooses all gone, and the warriors getting ready to attack the Agency at daylight next morning—that very hour.   They immediately assembled in council to hear the news from Uintah, and continued to discuss the situation until within an hour of daybreak, when they sent him on to tell me that they wanted to hear me talk, and would come in early.

He also said that the Uncompahgres were highly pleased with his report of the Uintah council, and assured me that if I would make the same explanations to them that I had made to the Uintahs and White Rivers, it would allay their fears concerning the soldiers, and remove much of their dissatisfaction regarding other matters.

And so it proved. The council was long and tedious, but entirely harmonious, and the result quite as satisfactory as it was at Uintah. We adjourned with the public promise from Saponero—given with the sanction of the entire council—that if my representations proved true, we should have the support instead of the hostility of the Uncompahgres, and that in any event if anything went wrong he would come and tell me or McKewen about it.

At 12 o'clock I started on the return trip to Uintah. About half way we met five Indians coming from Uintah as fast as their ponies could carry them. As they drew near and signalled to us to stop, we saw that they had been riding hard and were greatly excited. It gave me a very painful shock. I was afraid some new trouble had occurred at Uintah.

The leader was an old head man named Sour, whom Davis and I both knew to be one of the best disposed Indians on the Reservation. But he was now terribly excited. He did not wait to get nearer than a hundred yards to begin shouting:

"Buffalo soldiers! Buffalo soldiers! Coming. Maybe so to-morrow. Indians saw them at Burnt Fort yesterday, coming this way. Don't let them come! We can't stand it! It's bad—very bad!"

When he got up to us he continued to talk rapidly, both orally and by signs. He gave Davis no time to interpret, and perhaps said as much in five minutes with his mouth and hands together as could have been interpreted literally in half an hour. As soon as Davis could break in he gave me the substance of it as follows:

"You did not tell us that 'buffalo soldiers' were coming, and we did not agree for them to come. We did not think about them at all. Our agreement applies only to white soldiers. That is all right. We told you they might come, and they may. But all the Indians want you to come back quick and meet the 'buffalo soldiers' at the line and send them back. We cannot stand for them to come on our Reservation. It is too bad!"

I told Davis to ask him why the Indians objected to the colored troops, or "buffalo soldiers," as he called them. By this time he was too impatient and excited to wait on the interpreter. Leaping from his pony and rushing up to me as I sat in the buggy, he rubbed his hand briskly over my black coat sleeve and then over his face and exclaimed with great vehemence in broken English:

"*All over black! All over black, buffalo soldiers! Injun heap no like him!!*"

Then rubbing his head all over with a jerk of his hand, he almost screamed:

"*Woolly head! Woolly head! All same as buffalo! What you call him, black white man?* NIGGER! ! NIGGER ! ! !"

It took me an hour to get him calmed down and reconciled. I had not thought of colored troops myself, and was not aware that the Indians disliked them any more than they did white soldiers.

Finally, upon the assurance that all the soldier chiefs were white men, and the pledge of my word for the good conduct of the "buffaloes," Sour agreed that they might come, and gave me his word that he would hurry back and satisfy all the Indians.

At the Agency I found that Sour's excitement had been shared in by the entire tribe. I was also informed that the Utes had a strange and irreconcilable antipathy to negroes. Up to that time they had never suffered one to live on their Reservation. Several had dropped in among them from time to time in the past, but only to soon disappear and never be heard of again.

That afternoon General Crook arrived on the Reservation with four companies of infantry, and established the Post of Fort DuChesne.

The Indians watched this small force from all the high points, and showed considerable nervousness, but when they saw them go into camp, or "sit down," as they expressed it, at the place I had suggested, on the road and near halfway between the two Agencies, they told me again that it was all right—that they might "sit" there as long as they pleased, but they did not want them to come any nearer.

Early next morning the "buffalo soldiers"—four troops of colored cavalry—arrived. During the day a great many Indians came to talk with me about them, and many were the intimations in substance that if they did not stay pretty close to their wickiups they would certainly "hear something drop."

CHAPTER XVIII.

A FRESH ALARM AT UINTAH — A VISIT TO THE "SOL-
DIER CAMP" — A TERRIBLE NIGHT RIDE — THE END
OF OUR TROUBLES.

ABOUT 9 o'clock the second night after the arrival of the "buffaloes," an unusual commotion was heard over in Sowawick's village and among the scattering camps near the Agency.

Loud shouting could be plainly heard, and an employe who understood the language said runners were riding at full speed through the camps giving the alarm that soldiers were coming, and summoning the Indians to a council at Sowawick's camp immediately.

I was satisfied that a new excitement had broken out, but as our preparations for defense were as complete as we could make them, there was nothing we could do but await developments.

We had not long to wait. In less than half an hour I heard a great clatter of unshod hoofs approaching at full speed. They dashed up to my yard gate and stopped. Moccasined feet came running on the walk to the porch. There was a rush against my room door, and half a dozen Indians commenced pounding on it and shouting:

"Agent, soldiers! Agent, soldiers! Coming now! Maybe so *buffalo* soldiers!"

Opening the door, I asked them what was the matter. There were six or seven of them, all White Rivers, I thought, though Charlie Mack, the interpreter, was the only one whom I knew by name. He was a full-blood White River, and lived in Sowawick's village. They were so excited that they could hardly talk. When Charlie Mack became steady enough to talk with any coherency at all, it was as follows:

"Soldiers! Pony soldiers! Maybe so *buffalo* soldiers. Comin' now. Injuns see 'em at Antero's little bit ago. Injuns run fast and tell Sowawick. Maybe so comin' to catch Injuns to-night. Dunno, Injuns think so. All de Injuns heap scared. Squaws and pappooses all runnin' to mountains now. All de Injuns fight to-night—*right now*—*purty quick*. Sowawick send us to ask you what you say, *quick?*"

This was a stunner. Antero's camp was five miles down the road towards Camp DuChesne, and I could not understand myself why soldiers should be riding about on the Reservation, and especially coming to-

wards the Agency in the nighttime, without notice to
me.   I could not believe it true, and questioned Charlie
Mack again.   He said:

"Yes—since dark—little bit ago.   Injuns see 'em—
big band—comin' this way."

I was still incredulous, though Indians seldom make
mistakes in matters of that kind.   And true or false,
it was evident that something had to be done *quick*.
I could think of but one thing, and acted on it at once.
Speaking with decisiveness and energy, I said:

"Go back and tell Sowawick to send some of his
chiefs to go with me to see where the soldiers are going,
and what they are after.   I know they are not coming
to catch the Indians.   Maybe they are coming to see
me.   Maybe they are looking for lost horses.   I don't
know.   We will go and find out.   Some of you go and
tell Big Tom to come too.   Tell Sowawick to keep
the Indians quiet until we get back.   Go now, quick."

They ran out to their ponies, sprang to their backs
and sped away as if they expected the "buffalo soldiers" to catch the hindmost.

I ordered out the two best horses at the Agency,
and sent for Frank Boan, a brave young fellow originally from Illinois or Missouri, I do not recollect which.
I told him that the Indians would expect me to ride at
the front, but that he must ride at the rear, and in no

case permit any Indian to get behind him; that we would take four pistols apiece, and if fired on we would try to get together and make our way back to the Agency or to the Post.

By the time we were ready Charlie Mack had returned with Big Tom, Snake John, Bob Ridley and seven other chiefs. They brought word from Sowawick that no harm should be done to the Agency during our absence. Nevertheless, I charged all the employes to assemble at a designated house and stay together until we got back.

It was about 10 o'clock when we started. I put Big Tom back with Boan, and made Charlie Mack, the interpreter, ride with me.

When we got to Antero's camp, we found it deserted. The condition of the bedding and other things showed that it had been abandoned in great haste. The Indians concluded that the entire band had been captured, and became greatly excited. They proposed to turn back, but I told them that we would go on to the Post and make inquiry there. That steadied them somewhat, and we fell into the road again.

All along the route, and especially between the Agency and Antero's, we were frequently intercepted by Indians, most of whom seemed to be riding off a hundred yards or more from the road. They would first hail and get an answer in Indian, and then gallop in to ascertain who we were and where we were going. Several arose from the sagebrush right at the side of the road, where they were squatted as lookouts for the soldiers. They all looked wild and excited. They had heard of the troops and were hunting for them themselves, though not one of them had seen a soldier, or knew anything about Antero's band.

I kept the Indians talking to each other up and down the line in their own language, to avoid being mistaken for cavalry and fired on.

After passing Antero's camp the Indians rode exasperatingly slow, and as we neared the Post they hung back so much that I feared they would break away and not go up at all. It was evident that they were uneasy and suspicious of entrapment.

The moon was just fairly above the mesa to the east as we came in sight of the white tents in the valley. There was perfect silence in the camp, but we could see the sentinels walking their beats, apparently wide awake and vigilant. A dim light was burning in the guard tent on the corner that we were approaching, and a few men sitting near it.

The Indians were in single file, and had dropped back perhaps ten steps apart, making quite a long line. The low moon cast our shadows out over the plain, making us, as the sentinels said, look like a regiment of phantoms.

The sand being deep, our approach was noiseless, and we were within sixty yards before the guards discovered us.   Suddenly the men at the tent sprang to their feet and we heard the click-click of half a dozen rifles, and saw their bright barrels gleaming straight at us.   To the quick, energetic command: "Halt! Who goes there?" I made prompt answer, and told Charlie Mack to interpret everything to the Indians.   The Sergeant asked me to wait where we were until he could wake the commanding officer.   While he was gone we rode a few steps to one side and hitched our horses to the cottonwood trees on the bank of the river.   In a few minutes the Sergeant returned with word from the commanding officer to come to his tent, which was situated in the center of the camp.

At the guard tent a file of soldiers with guns closed up on each side of us, with the Sergeant in front, to escort us to the commanding officer's quarters.   As the soldiers appeared on both sides of us, I looked back at the Indians, who were following me in single file, with Boan still at the rear.   They were the most solemn and worst hoodooed-looking human beings I ever saw. I doubt if any of them had much hope of ever getting out of the camp alive.   Fortunately, the soldiers were white. If they had been "buffaloes," I am sure the Indians would have stampeded in spite of all we could have done.

General Crook had that day started back to Omaha, leaving Captain J. W. Duncan, of the Twenty-First Infantry, in temporary command. He and Lieutenants John S. Parke and H. L. Bailey and several other officers had jerked on their uniforms and swords, and were tumbling things around to make room for us. I introduced all the Indians to Captain Duncan by name, and explained the cause of our visit at that inconvenient and unusual hour.

Captain Duncan assured the Indians that a mistake had been made; that all of his men had answered to roll call at sunset, and he was sure none of them had left camp since. At my request he also gave them substantially the same explanations and assurances that I had given at Uintah and Ouray, and from being the worst frightened they soon became the best pleased Indians I ever saw. They talked a few minutes among themselves, and then Charlie Mack told us that they had concluded that "maybe some Injun heap scared and see some cowboys or some ghoses, like white man, and think they soldiers."

As soon as we had passed the guard tent going out, the Indians said good-bye to me and Boan, mounted and started back as fast as their ponies could carry them, not one waiting or even looking back for another.

It was 8 o'clock when Boan and I got back to the Agency, and we were completely exhausted, having had a really terrible all-night ride of thirty-five miles without sleep, rest or refreshment of any kind, not even a drink of good water, to say nothing of the strain of excitement and apprehension.

We found everything quiet at the Agency and in all the Indian camps. In fact Sowawick had discovered the mistake long before our return. A boy herder of Antero's band saw a squad of Uncompahgres coming up from Ouray, and mistaking them in the dark for soldiers, he ran back to camp and gave the alarm, whereat Antero and his entire band struck out afoot across country to Big Tom's camp, and arrived there shortly after our departure.

This trip established me firmly in the confidence of the Indians, and there was never any more excitement or trouble of any kind with them during my term as Acting Agent.

CHAPTER XIX.

THE SIOUX VISIT THE UTES — A BIG DOG FEAST —
THREE HUNDRED INDIANS DANCING AT ONE TIME
— AN EXTRAORDINARY DISPLAY OF PAINT, FEATH-
ERS AND SLEIGH BELLS.

AS the excitement and war talk subsided the Indians
resumed their regular pastimes, which consist
largely of horse racing, dancing and card playing.

The three bands own upwards of twelve thousand
ponies, many of them being really fine horses. Straight
stretches of wagon road serve as race tracks, the usual
distance being about five hundred yards. Being fond
of bunch races, they will enter as many ponies as can
find room on the track, or within twenty yards of it,
and for any amount from a pistol cartridge to the largest
bunch of ponies on the Reservation.

At cards they are wonderfully expert—more so, I
have heard competent white men say, than "the heathen
Chinee." One of their principal games is what is
known in that region as Mexican monte, and the other

is poker, though cowboys used to tell me that even the latter is so thoroughly Indianized as to be a perfect hoodoo to a white man.

They have no regular places for playing, but wherever two or three are gathered together there a blanket and a deck of cards may be seen also.   The blanket is spread on the ground—in the shade if one happens to be convenient, if not, then in the blazing sun—and the game begins, and generally to be continued for many hours.

The women also gamble with one another, and sometimes win and lose large stakes.   A very thrifty Indian living near the Agency had two good tents, several valuable robes and blankets, an abundance of wearing apparel and other household goods suitable to their mode of life.   One day during his absence his squaw gambled off both tents and every solitary thing they contained, except herself and two pappooses.   When he returned at night he found her happily sojourning with a neighbor, the tents and all their contents having been promptly removed by the winner.   The incident resulted in no domestic disturbance, however.   The husband expressed some contempt for his wife's skill and judgment, but no disapproval of her habit of playing and betting.

Unlike white men, Indians rarely ever have trouble

with one another over their games. They will gamble at cards and run horse races every day for months without even a quarrel. I do not recollect to have ever heard of but two or three altercations resulting from racing or card playing.

For a ball room they sometimes have a tepee, sometimes a bush wickiup, and sometimes the open prairie. A full orchestra is composed of a bass drum, at least two tom-toms, and three or four of a wooden instrument the name of which I never heard. The tom-tom is a small drum made by stretching wet rawhide over the top of a camp kettle, or other thing of that shape. The wooden instrument is made of hard wood in the form of a chair rocker, with notches on the inverted edge. The musician rubs the notches with a cobblestone, and the effect is enough to make a white man dance—with frenzy. The drums are placed on the ground, and as many Indians as can get in reach pound on them leisurely, but with unvarying stroke, from beginning to end, while a chorus of squaws sing: "Ki-yi, ko-yo, ki-yi, ko-yo, ki-yi, ko-yo-ko." A full orchestra, however, is not indispensable to a successful Ute "german." Frequently only one instrument is used.

The different tribes are also fond of visiting each other in large numbers, and Agents frequently find it inexpedient to refuse them permission to do so, even if they can see no benefit to be derived from it.

About three weeks after the abatement of the trouble at Uintah, over four hundred Ogalalla Sioux came down from Pine Ridge Agency, in South Dakota, on a visit to the Utes. They were all men, and many of them well advanced in years. The leader was a young man who gave his name as Red Cloud, and claimed to be a son of the noted Sioux chief of that name. They came direct to the office, presented their papers, and requested an issue of rations from the Ute supplies.

They had a great many papers of the nature of testimonials, or certificates of good character, but the only pass was one issued by the Army officer then Acting Agent at Pine Ridge for "the bearer and a few friends" to visit the Shoshone Agency, in Wyoming. Upon the inch contained in that paper the entire party had slipped off to Shoshone, and after stopping there a few days, had taken the ell of three hundred and fifty miles to Uintah. The distance from Pine Ridge to Uintah by way of Shoshone is not less than nine hundred miles. The ponies were badly jaded, and the Indians themselves looked gaunt and hungry.

Of course they had to admit that their visit was unauthorized in writing, but they insisted that they had verbal permission, and to convince me that they were on a peaceable mission they led their pack ponies to the office door and unloaded over a hundred long-stem

(6)

pipes, made of the Dakota red pipestone, and large quantities of moccasins, tobacco pouches and other trinkets made of buckskin and ornamented with beads and porcupine quills, which they said they had brought to "swap" to the Utes for ponies and buckskin.

Being satisfied that their "excursion," whether authorized or not, was only for pleasure and the exchange of gifts with the Utes, and seeing also that it would be impossible for them to recruit their ponies for the return trip under a week, I consented for them to remain that long, but told them that they would have to look to the Utes themselves for beef and flour.   With many grunts expressive of deep satisfaction, they hurried off to see the Ute chiefs, who came in an hour or two later and asked for an advance issue of six beeves and other supplies for their visitors, who they said were "heap hungry."

Three or four days later the Ute chiefs came to the office again and gave me a formal and very pressing invitation to a big dog feast, which they said they were going to give the Ogalallas at Sowawick's camp the next day.   Lieutenant John S. Parke, of the Army, happening to be at the Agency, I introduced them to him, and they invited him also.   Upon what we understood to be an assurance that we would not be expected to partake of the feast unless it was entirely agreeable to us, we both promised to go.

At 9 o'clock next morning Parke and I mounted our horses and rode across the creek to the camp. All of the Uintahs and White Rivers, several hundred of the Uncompahgres, and the four hundred Sioux—at least two thousand in all—had already assembled, and were nearly ready to begin the feast They were all in excellent humor, and seemed to be enjoying the occasion about as white people usually enjoy a Fourth of July barbecue.

Near the center of the camp a round spot perhaps one hundred feet in diameter had been scraped off as smooth as a brickyard, to serve the double purpose of ball room and banquet hall. It seemed that the Indians had been waiting for Parke and myself, and we were given seats of honor with the chiefs on a carpet of blankets and robes spread on a little knoll at the edge of the ring.

The tom-toms were immediately sounded to call the dancers from their wickiups, where they had been making their "toilets," of which paint, feathers and sleigh bells were the most conspicuous articles. There were at least three hundred of them—all men, some of the women singing, but none dancing.

Indians use the bright colored paints—green, blue, red, yellow and white—to enhance their beauty, and the young bucks, or dudes, as the white boys call them, spread it on thick when they go courting, or into the dance. And as this was an extraordinary occasion, they had used their brushes with extraordinarily lavish hands. One had the whole of one eye painted a bright yellow, and the other a brilliant green. His forehead was a blue field with a white star in the center. One side of his face was ornamented with green and yellow stripes, and the other with red, white and blue stars. He is described in detail, however, only to give the reader an idea of how they all looked, for his face was not painted more fantastically than scores of others, and no two were alike.

Each dancer wore from two to seven bands of sleigh bells—a band of large ones around the waist, and smaller ones around the ankles, knees and arms. Think of three hundred men dancing with from two to seven bands of sleigh bells of various sizes buckled around them so as to jingle with every motion of the body! Such a sound is as animating to an Indian camp as the Marine Band's "Star Spangled Banner" or "Dixie" is to an assemblage of white people.

The dancers seemed to go through certain figures, the time required to dance a set being about twenty minutes. At the end of the first one Sowawick stepped into the center of the ring and made what seemed from his gestures and modulations of voice to be a speech of general felicitation to the Utes and of friendship and hospitality to the Sioux, though of course we could not understand anything he said. He was responded to by one of the Sioux chiefs in what was clearly a speech of congratulation and good will. They both used signs as well as oral delivery, so that all might understand, for the Utes and Sioux could not converse with each other except by the sign language, which is the universal language of the plains Indians.

They continued alternately speaking and dancing until 12 o'clock. At that hour the chief of the feast, a "medicine man" named Wash, entered the ring and made some sort of a proclamation, which drew all the Indians in camp still closer around the ring, and produced perfect silence. The dancers—of whom perhaps one hundred were Sioux and two hundred Utes—sat down around the edge of the ring. Two camp kettles full of steaming meat were brought from the fires and placed immediately in front of the "grand stand"—that is, the knoll occupied by the chiefs, Parke and myself. Two squaws brought some small dishes and filled them with the stewed meat, which had been cut into pieces about three-quarters of an inch square before being cooked.

The chief of the feast took one of the dishes, came up on the knoll, made a short speech, which seemed to be a sort of grace or invocation, and extended the dish to Sowawick. Sowawick, taking out a piece of the meat with his fingers, and holding it up before his face, said a few words in a reverent or ceremonious manner, dropped the morsel into his mouth, chewed a time or two, swallowed with some difficulty, batted his eyes, and then looked around with an expression of countenance which seemed to say: "That's the way to do it; follow my example." All the chiefs and dancers grunted enthusiastic applause.

The same ceremony was repeated with the Sioux chief, and then Wash turned to *me!* Parke and I had been joking each other considerably, but thinking that we had been excused in advance by the chiefs, we did not expect any serious embarrassment. The chiefs all gathered around, however, and made us understand by signs and a few words of broken English, that as we were their friends they would be deeply grieved if we did not partake of the feast with them!

I had recognized Charlie Mack among the dancers, and seeing him sitting not far away laughing at us, I called to him to come and help us out of our dilemma. The rascal was making no concealment of his enjoyment of our embarrassment, and instead of coming to our assistance he said:

"No; me one of de dancers. Me have to stay here

now.   You jis eat it some dog; dat's all dey want.
Sowawick he tell de Sioux you his friend.   I speck it
good.   Maybe me eat lots of it.   You tase it; maybe you like it.   Fattest kind o' dog.   Yaller dog.
One ear cut off.   Me see him yistiddy.''

I brought him to terms, however, with a threat to
strike his name from the issue roll of the tribe, and after
he had spoken a few words to the Indians he said:

"Dat's all right.   I tell 'em you no like it dog; dat
white man dunno what's good nohow.''

The chiefs grunted their satisfaction with his explanation, and resuming their seats they were served just
as Sowawick and Red Cloud had been, each receiving
hearty applause as he swallowed his morsel.   Two
other "medicine men'' entered the ring and assisted
Wash to administer to the dancers.

When the ceremonies at the ring were ended the
crowd scattered out in groups around the fires in all
parts of the camp and the feast on fresh beef and dog
meat became general.

CHAPTER XX.

A LITTLE SAVAGE IN SCHOOL—HAVOC AND CONSTER-
NATION AMONG THE LADIES—A TENDERFOOT ON A
BICYCLE—ROPING AND BRANDING BEEF CATTLE AT
OURAY—ASTONISHING FEATS OF THE CHAMPION
"ROPER" OF UTAH.

MISS FANNIE A. WEEKS, of Florida, was
superintendent of the Reservation school at
Uintah. Mrs. Clara Granger, of Salt Lake City, was
matron, and Mrs. Annie R. Morgan, of Kentucky, was
seamstress. They were most excellent ladies, and ad-
mirably adapted to their respective places.

The Uncompahgres could not be induced to send
any of their children to school, but by great energy and
perseverance Miss Weeks had gathered in nearly thirty
very nice little Uintahs and White Rivers, and she was
quite proud of them. I was much inclined to help her,
and urged the Indians to bring in as many children as
she could accommodate.

One day an Indian whom the employes had given
the name of John Duncan, brought me his little boy—

an exceptionally fine specimen of the juvenile savage. He was about seven years old, and dressed in a full suit of painted, beaded and fringed buckskin, including moccasins. He had probably never been left alone with a white person a minute in his life, and was almost as wild as a jack rabbit. Giving him some candy, I told his father to take him on to the school, only a little over a hundred yards distant.

In a short while John returned with a note from Miss Weeks in which she thanked me for causing the boy to be brought in, and stated that she and Mrs. Granger and Mrs. Morgan were in ecstacies over him, he was "*so* cute" in his little suit of buckskin, and had already named him in my honor.

John sat down to tell me what a nice boy he was. He was still describing his precociousness when I heard a tremendous disturbance break out up at the school-house. Tables and chairs were being hurled about, women were screaming, children were running in every direction, and in a moment Mrs. Morgan came flying out of the house shouting to me to come quick, that that "little hyena" was just killing Miss Weeks and Mrs. Granger.

I ran to their rescue, of course, with John following at my heels. In the main study room we found the two ladies and my little namesake, now alluded to as a "little hyena." Miss Weeks is an obese lady and of mature years, and she was now too excited and short of breath to talk—absolutely speechless. In fact she was almost in a swoon, and looked as if a hyena had been toying with her sure enough. Her dress was torn, her face badly scratched, and two-thirds of her hair missing. In another part of the room Mrs. Granger stood trying to stanch a strong flow of blood from her nose. She seemed to be even more hopelessly wrecked than Miss Weeks. Her dress was, as she expressed it, "just *ruined*," the few short tufts of hair that she had left from a beautiful suit looked "just shocking," her face and neck showed several ugly fingernail scratches, one ear was bitten almost off, and her nose was swollen to ridiculous size, and bleeding profusely. Crouched on top of a high wood-box in one corner of the room was Master Eugene Duncan, the worst scared little animal I ever saw. As soon as Miss Weeks could speak she shouted:

"Take that little wildcat away from here! Take him away!"

"Oh, I should hate to do that," I said; "he seems '*so* cute.' Why, he just seems to have you and Mrs. Granger *in ecstacies!*"

That made them both so mad that they had to sit down and take "a good cry." When they had washed their faces, swept the hair and other debris from the floor, and got in a good humor, they gave me the particulars of the combat, which, they said, came up quite unexpectedly to them. When John left the boy with them they petted him awhile, gave him nice things to eat, and tried to get him to talk to them, which of course he could not do, not being able to speak or understand a word of English. Finally Miss Weeks turned her attention to something else in another part of the house, and Mrs. Granger started to take him to the storeroom to exchange his buckskin for a suit of clothes. When she stooped to take his hand, the little fellow sprang up on her shoulders and went to scratching, biting and pulling hair like a real wildcat. Of course, when Miss Weeks heard the screaming she rushed heroically to the rescue of Mrs. Granger. In trying to pull the boy loose she bent Mrs. Granger over on a table. The little Indian jumped off on the table kicked Mrs. Granger on the nose, leaped up on Miss Weeks' shoulders and commenced to pluck her head. She struggled and screamed tremendously at first, but in a little while she dropped on her hands and knees and commenced to pray. When she sank entirely to the floor the little fellow jumped off, ran to the far corner of the room and climbed up on the wood-box. The ladies said he did not utter a word—did not even whimper—during the melee, and did not look at all mad, but just seemed to be scared almost to death.

At my request John stayed with him until next day, by which time he had become reconciled and gentle, and in ten days he was a pet of the superintendent and matron, and regarded by all as one of the brightest and most amiable children in the school.

Soon after this episode I spent nearly two weeks at Ouray, receiving beef cattle. The contract required the year's supply to be furnished at one delivery about the first of October. Mr. McAndrews, the chief herder, was a very careful man, and required every animal to be thrown, so that it could be thoroughly branded.

This afforded me opportunity to witness some very fine work with the lasso, and many excellent feats of horsemanship. Mr. Gidney, one of the herders, was the champion "roper" of several States and Territories, having taken the premium and medal at the Denver Exposition the year before.

To throw the cattle the herders would all mount their trained cow-ponies and ride into the corral. One of them would rope a steer by the horns and take a hitch on a snubbing post, which was firmly set in the ground in the center of the corral. The others would start him to running and then one of them would catch him by the hind legs. The latter throw generally fell to Gidney, as it was the most difficult.   He seldom failed to catch one leg, and I think at least three times in five he would get both.

Having the steer by both legs he would quickly wind the rope around the horn of his saddle and ride straight away from the snubbing post.   The steer being thus stretched out and tripped behind, he would soon fall over on his side perfectly helpless.   The branding irons were heated outside by Indian laborers.   The very instant the steer was "tied down" they were on top of him with the red hot irons, and the louder he bawled the better they enjoyed it.

The greatest danger was in turning the steers loose after they were branded, for by that time they were thoroughly infuriated.   Carefully holding his horns and feet until both ropes were removed, all hands would spring to their horses or the corral fence, and sometimes it was a close race with some of them, for the steer never failed to make a furious dash for the first one he caught sight of on getting to his feet.

I have seen a great deal of rope work, but that was the best.   To the man who has never tried it, such work being done by a skillful roper may appear quite easy.   But whenever a tenderfoot undertakes himself to throw and tie down a big, wild, long-horned steer in an open corral, he soon finds that he needs the help of the whole neighborhood. The Ouray boys worked very hard, and branded considerably over a hundred a day.

About this time a young fellow from New York came along on a trip across the continent on a bicycle, on a race against the time made by another bicyclist some years before.

The road across the Reservation was not one of the main traveled roads from Denver to Salt Lake City. On the contrary it was in some places merely a trail. But having ascertained somehow that it was nearer than the other routes, he had recklessly plunged into it. The Reservation was not shown on his map, however, and he said he did not know there was an Indian in the United States outside of the Indian Territory. Nobody had thought to tell him about the Utes, all supposing that he knew where they were. The Agency being marked on his map as "White Rocks," he supposed it was an ordinary ranch or village, and was making for it as a stopping place for the night.

On the road he was traveling there was not a house to be seen—not even a permanent Indian camp—between the line of the Reservation and the Agency, a distance of forty miles. But a mile and a half from the Agency the Indians had just the day before completed a large bush wickiup in the form of a horseshoe, with the open heel to the road, and only a few feet from it.

This wickiup being simply a wall of green willow bushes six or seven feet high closely wattled together, it looked at a casual glance just like a willow thicket, and the bicycle man thought it was. But there were two hundred Utes inside, and at least one hundred and fifty of them dancing.

As the sun was fast disappearing behind the mountains, the traveler was straining his eyes for a sight of White Rocks, fearing that if darkness overtook him on the plain he might lose the road and be devoured by coyotes. Hearing a noise he slowed up to listen. Recognizing it as human voices, he thought there must be a settlement behind the clump of willows, and pushed on.

Slowing up as he caught a glimpse of the people inside, he had come to a full stop in front of the wickiup before he saw that they were Indians. The Indians seeing him at the same instant, they came rushing out and crowded around him so closely that he could not move. He had never seen an Indian, and they had never even heard of a bicycle. And there they were— face to face! The Indians were simply amazed; the white man was absolutely terror-stricken. He sat completely paralyzed with fright until one of the Indians asked him a question in English. That brought him back to consciousness sufficiently to say: "White Rocks —White Rocks."

Seeing that he was scared nearly to death, the Indians stood out of his way and told him to go on.   Although he did not have to be told a second time, he was too weak and nervous to go fast; and, to make the case worse for him, thirty or forty of the Indians jumped on their ponies and followed close behind him, partly to see how he got along on the wheel, and partly to see if he stopped at White Rocks.

When the man arrived at the Agency he was almost delirious.   Doctor Williams administered sedatives to him, but he tossed restlessly on his couch all night, and for several hours any unusual noise would startle him so that an employe had to stay in the room with him to keep him from jumping up and running off.

About sunrise next morning fifteen or twenty of the chiefs of both bands appeared at the office for a council. It was evident from their appearances that they had been up all night.   They said they had come to ask me to make the man with the ''iron pony'' go right on. Of course I knew that he intended to go anyhow, but to satisfy my curiosity I asked them why they did not want him to stop.   They replied:

''Because we never saw a pony like that before, and we will not run our ponies against it.   It is not like our ponies, and we do not know how fast it can run.   It has no feet, no mouth, no get breath, maybe so no get tired. Injun dunno. Maybe so white man want to heap win him Injun money and pony. Dunno. Injun think so. You make him go on. No let him sit down here. Injun no run it any more horse race until he gets off the Reservation.''

It was evident that they believed the bicycle was an ''iron race-horse'' that the man had brought there to run against their ponies. But he had even less use for them than they did for him, and twenty minutes after their arrival they had the satisfaction of seeing him depart. At Salt Lake City he gave the newspaper reporters a breezy, four-column account of the incident, which they printed under half a column of displayed headlines.

CHAPTER XXI.

A TRIP TO SALT LAKE CITY—ON THE ROOF OF A
SQUATTER'S "DUGOUT"—THROUGH DEEP AND
NARROW CANYONS — WONDERFUL ECHOES—UTAH
LAKE, JORDAN RIVER AND GREAT SALT LAKE—SALT
LAKE CITY—RETURN TO THE AGENCY.

IN the latter part of October I was required to make
a trip to Salt Lake City, to hurry up the delivery
of the annual supplies at Uintah and Ouray before the
roads became blockaded with snow, the small creeks
being already frozen over.

Deciding to take Mr. McKewen with me, we agreed
to meet at Fort DuChesne and start to the railroad from
that place.   He came up to the Post in the afternoon
of October 31st, and I arranged to start at 2 o'clock in
the morning and get there for breakfast.

Mr. Hemsworth, the farmer, was to take me.   Calling
me at 1:30, as directed, he made the unwelcome announcement that it was "snowing to beat creation,"
and suggested that we take a span of nimble-footed

mules, instead of horses, as they could travel in the snow with less difficulty, to which I assented.

We started at 2 o'clock.   The snow was then three or four inches deep, and still falling beautifully.   A mile from the Agency the road crosses a creek, one of the main branches of the little Uintah River.   A dense thicket of willows and grease wood extends entirely across the bottom on both sides of the road.   Until we came to the bottom the mules, mule like, kept trying to quit the road and turn back, but when we got in between the walls of the bush we felt no further danger of losing our way.

The creek had low, sloping banks, and I remembered afterwards that the road ran diagonally across it. When we had been driving long enough, as I thought, to be entirely across the bottom I remarked to Hemsworth that we seemed to be a long time getting to the creek.   Being of an exceedingly sanguine temperament, he whipped up the team and replied:

"No; we've hardly got that far yet.   We'll come to it pretty soon.   These blamed mules don't like to take the snow."

I knew, however, that we were traveling at the rate of five or six miles an hour, and I could also tell that we were making a great many abrupt turns that I had never noticed in the road.   Fifteen or twenty minutes later I happened to think or notice that the buggy had ceased to jolt against the cobblestones, and that the road seemed to be as smooth and soft as a carpeted floor. I was sure we had traveled at least five or six miles, and told Mr. Hemsworth so. He still thought we would come to the creek in a little while, and gave the mules several vigorous cuts with the whip, pushing them into a brisk trot.

Striking a match and holding it to my watch, I showed Mr. Hemsworth that we had been traveling an hour and twenty minutes. He was excitable and impulsive as well as sanguine. Throwing his whole weight back on the reins, he exclaimed:

"Whoa! Well, great cæsar! Where do you suppose these dog-gone mules is takin' us?"

Jumping out of the buggy and feeling around in the snow with our hands, we discovered, to Mr. Hemsworth's unspeakable amazement, that we were traveling in the channel of the creek on the ice. The willow and grease wood bushes were bent over by the snow until there was just room·enough to drive in the center of the channel.

One of us lifting the hind wheels of the buggy around while the other turned the team, we started back to find the road. Mr. Hemsworth was greatly exercised to know whether we had gone up stream or down. Neither of us could tell, and, of course, without knowing that, we would not know which end of the road to take when we found it.

In a short while we came to a small opening on the banks, and Mr. Hemsworth got out to feel for the road. It was not there, and he reported that the snow, which was still falling furiously, had already obliterated the tracks we had made in going down. We continued an hour and a half in that direction, stopping frequently to feel for the road, and then concluding that we had passed it, we turned back.

And thus we continued to drive up and down the creek until daylight revealed the Agency to us not exceeding a mile away. Mr. Hemsworth swore it was on the wrong side of the creek, and would not believe it was the Agency. But taking bearings from it anyhow, we soon found the road and resumed our journey to the Post, arriving there at 9 o'clock, the distance from the Agency being estimated at twelve miles.

After a short stop for breakfast, Mr. McKewen and I took the road to Price Station, on the Denver & Rio Grande Railroad, ninety miles distant, with the Ouray team, a span of large horses. At 12 o'clock we stopped at DuChesne River for lunch.

There is not a drop of water between DuChesne River and Minnie Maud Creek, in Nine Mile Canyon, a distance of forty-two miles. Neither of us had ever been over the road before, but we had been informed that we could get accommodations for the night at Brock's, whose place we would find in the canyon, on the bank of Minnie Maud Creek. Nobody had thought to tell us what sort of a place it was, and of course we both expected to see a house. It was 10 o'clock at night when we arrived at the creek. Seeing no house, we hallooed, but received no answer, except the wonderful echo, which alone seemed loud enough to wake the sleeping for miles around. Turning to one side we drove up on a low bluff overlooking a little valley in a bend of the creek. Stopping at the very brink of the bluff we hallooed again. Quick as a flash a man darted right out from beneath our horses' feet. Running out about fifteen steps in front, he whirled around, threw up his hands wildly, and fairly shrieked:

"What in the thunderation you doin' up there on top o' my house? Git down from there quick, or I'll shoot your dog-goned heads off!"

It was Brock—or *Mr.* Brock, as we were very particular to call him—whose house was merely a "dug-out," the back end being level with the surface, and the front flush with the face of the bluff. The dirt roof was supported by a layer of cottonwood poles. We had driven out on the roof at the rear end and stopped within a foot of the front edge, immediately over the door.

When Brock got through saying things to us, which it took him some time to do, he told us that he was asleep in a chair by his little sheet-iron stove when he was suddenly awakened by our halloo, and hearing the roof poles cracking, and a great shower of clods falling on him at the same instant, he thought the roof was falling in.   Of course he was badly frightened, and he said that when he got outside and saw our horses outlined against the sky they looked as tall as giraffes and as big as elephants.

When I ventured to express my opinion of a white man who would live alone in "a hole in the ground" there in that lonely canyon, Mr. Brock admitted that he was doing it for revenue and not for pleasure.   Being the only settler on the road, and situated midway between the railroad and the two Agencies, Fort DuChesne and the town of Ashley, he had a monopoly of considerable traffic.   He kept all sorts of forage and supplies, and no traveler or freighter could very well pass in either direction without spending some money with him.

Between DuChesne River and Price there are nearly thirty miles of canyons, and in many places they are so narrow and crooked, and their walls so high and steep, that everywhere the road seems to be abutting squarely against a vertical wall only a few yards ahead.

In such places there are wonderful echoes.   A loud

halloo will reverberate from cliff to cliff and come back to the listener in a great wave of echoes from a hundred different directions, and when they have almost died away in the distance, they gather volume and come back again, to be followed that time by an awful stillness and silence.

From Price we had a delightful daylight run to Salt Lake City, arriving there about the middle of the afternoon. At Provo the traveler gets a fair view of Utah Lake, a large fresh water lake situated nearly five thousand feet above the sea. From the north end of Utah Lake the railroad follows the meanderings of the Jordan River of the Mormons to Salt Lake City. The Jordan River has a swift current, and draws off the waters of Utah Lake, of which it is the only outlet, and pours them into the Great Salt Lake. These two lakes—one fresh and the other salt, or "dead"—and their connecting river are remarkable counterparts of the Sea of Galilee, the Dead Sea, and the Jordan River of the Holy Land.

The Great Salt Lake is one hundred miles long by sixty miles wide, and has an average depth of forty feet. Its surface is four thousand four hundred feet above the sea, and it has no known outlet. Three fresh water rivers, the Jordan, the Weber, the Bear, and several smaller streams fed by springs and melting snows in the mountains, empty into it, and yet its waters contain more than twenty-five per cent of salt in solution, for which reason it is said that there is not a fish or other living thing in it. The water is remarkably clear and transparent, and so heavy that a human body will not sink in it.

Salt Lake City is situated on the plain at the base of the Wahsatch Mountains, seven miles from the lake. It is the capital of the Territory, and also the chief city of the Mormons, by whom it was founded when they were driven from Nauvoo, Illinois, in 1847, Utah at that time being Mexican territory.

It is a picturesque and delightful city, and in many respects unlike any other in the United States. It was laid out on a liberal scale, and has over a hundred miles of streets one hundred and twenty feet wide. The blocks are six hundred and sixty feet square, and a stream of clear water and a row of shade trees line each side of most of the streets.

The famous Temple Block constitutes the heart, or center of the city. It contains the magnificent Mormon Temple, the celebrated Tabernacle, the mysterious Endowment House, and another church edifice known as the Assembly Hall.

The Temple is a magnificent edifice. It is built of granite, and is two hundred feet long and one hundred feet wide.   The walls are one hundred feet high, nine feet thick at the bottom and six feet at the top.   There are three towers at each end over two hundred feet high. The Mormons have been forty years building it, laying the corner stone in 1853, and dedicating it the present year, 1893.

The Tabernacle is chiefly remarkable perhaps on account of its peculiar shape, the roof being oval, or in the form of a turtle's back.   The Mormons claim that this is the largest roof in the world without central support.   It contains a million shingles, besides a large space at the apex covered with metal.   This Tabernacle, like the Temple, was built by Mormon architects, the prophets claiming that the plans of both buildings were revealed to them in visions.

The Endowment House is a one-story adobe cottage. It is situated in one corner of the Temple Block, and until the completion of the great Temple all the secret endowment rites of the church were performed within its walls.   I was told that no Gentile had ever seen inside of it.

The Tithing Office, where the tithes or church taxes are collected, is situated just across the street from the Temple Block.

Mr. McKewen and I spent three days in delightful recreation and sight-seeing in the city.   The visit would have been enjoyable to me at any time, but it was all the more so to us both on this occasion because of our long sojourn among the Utes on the Dry Tortugas, as Mr. McKewen called the Uncompahgre Reservation.

We were absent ten days, but upon our return to the Agency we found the Indians quiet, and everything moving along smoothly.

CHAPTER XXII.

RELIEVED AT UINTAH AND OURAY—DEPART FOR THE
INDIAN TERRITORY—SPEND TWO DAYS IN "ZION"
FRATERNIZING WITH THE "SAINTS"—THROUGH THE
GRAND CANYON AND ROYAL GORGE OF THE ARKAN-
SAS—A BLIZZARD AT DODGE CITY, KANSAS—A DEER
HUNT IN THE TERRITORY—TO OSAGE AGENCY.

AS soon as the disturbances at Uintah and Ouray
were abated the Department commenced to look
around for a permanent Agent.   But the Indians had
become so notorious that it was hard to find a suitable
man who would accept the place.   During the fall it
was declined by four different men.

The fifth appointee, Colonel Timothy A. Byrnes, of
New Jersey, had the nerve to accept, and wanted an
office too bad to decline.   He arrived in the latter part
of December, coming in from Green River, Wyoming,
on top of seven sacks of Christmas mail, on the wab-
bling little mail sled.

Being relieved by Colonel Byrnes on the first of January, I immediately departed for Muscogee, in the

Indian Territory, going by way of Salt Lake City, to which place I was accompanied by Mr. Clarence A. Granger, who had lived there several years, and was related to a number of prominent Mormon families.

Having become greatly attached to all of the employes and many of the Indians during my term of seven months at Uintah and Ouray, I bade them goodbye with deep and sincere regret, and in the earnest hope that I might some day meet them all again, a hope which I still entertain, but which we all knew then, as I feel now, is not likely ever to be realized.

Mr. Granger and I spent three days in "Zion" fraternizing with the "Saints," being the recipients of many courtesies and hospitalities from his Mormon relatives and friends, all of whom were highly intelligent and refined people, and with whom my brief acquaintance was extremely delightful.

From Salt Lake City I proceeded to the Indian Territory by way of the Denver & Rio Grande Railroad to Pueblo, Colorado; thence over the Sante Fe to Kansas City, and thence south on the M. K. & T. to Muscogee.

The Denver & Rio Grande claims to be the scenic route of the continent, and the scenery along its line is certainly very grand.   On the west side of the Rocky Mountains it passes through the famous Black Canyon of the Gunnison River, and on the east side it runs

ROYAL GORGE, Grand Canyon of the Arkansas.

through the Royal Gorge and Grand Canyon of the Arkansas River.

The Grand Canyon is seventeen miles long, and the Royal Gorge is so narrow, and the solid rock walls so high and steep, that a bridge of peculiar design had to be built through it over the channel of the river for the railroad track.   It is called the Devil's Bridge, and is said to be the only one of the kind in the world.   It is suspended from iron girders set in the walls of the gorge in the form of rafters.

At Dodge City, in Western Kansas, our train was caught in a blizzard—one of the worst ever known on the plains, and the first bad one I ever saw.

A tenderfoot once asked a distinguished United States Senator from Kansas what a blizzard was. "A blizzard, sir," replid the Senator, "is a cold wind, which, rising at the North Pole, moves south or south by southeast, through Manitoba, the Dakotas and Nebraska, increasing its velocity and intensifying its frigidity, until it reaches Kansas, when it will penetrate a three-foot brick wall, all the blankets that one family can get together, the thickest and most abundant clothing, pierce right through your flesh, and die away whistling Yankee Doodle through your marrow bones."

Colonel Pat Donan, in describing the suddenness with which blizzards usually make their appearance in the country, once narrated the following incident: "One morning toward the middle of January my old friend, Judge Willis Samuel, who lived down on Salt River, a stream of which you have probably heard, started to haul a heavy log to Hickman's sawmill, about two miles from his house. It was so warm that he was in his shirt sleeves, and only threw his coat up on the wagon because he knew the changeableness of the climate. As his oxen jogged along he passed a small pond near a crab apple thicket. The crab apple trees were budding, and the pond was literally swarming with frogs, all with their heads poked up and mouths wide open, singing like mud larks a joyous anthem to spring. By the time he reached the mill the wind had whipped around to the northwest, and it began to sleet and snow. Before he could get the log off his wagon it was bitterly cold and a blizzard raging. He jerked on his coat, borrowed a blanket, and started his oxen home at a swinging trot. In a few minutes he reached the pond he had passed, and there were all the poor little frogs, with their heads sticking through the ice and their mouths still open. The pond had frozen over so suddenly that the ice had caught them round their throats and choked them to death before they could pull their heads under or shut their mouths. It was a sad sight."

Of course I am not expected to vouch for anything

either Colonel Donan or a United States Senator has said or may say in reference to blizzards. To be entirely candid, I hardly think I could afford to do so. But the blizzard at Dodge City came upon us quite as suddenly as that one did upon Judge Samuel and the frogs, and was very much of the character of the one described by the Senator. As we went thundering along over the plains every car window was open. About 4 o'clock in the afternoon the sky became overcast. Almost at the same instant there came howling about the train a wind which seemed to be a breath direct from the arctic regions. Apparently with one movement every window was closed. Ten minutes later the passengers were calling for fire, and by the time that was done the cars were so darkened by frost on the window panes that lamps had to be lighted.

The clouds were dark and heavy, and seemed to come down entirely to the earth. The gale was blowing fifty miles or more an hour, and there was something that glittered and hissed and moaned and howled dolefully in the wind. It was not snow. It was colder than snow. It was not sleet. It was colder than sleet. It was not sheets of ice. It was colder than mere ice. It was glittering, bristling, spangled spears of *frost*, and wherever it fell on one's hands or face it seemed to sink right into the flesh without melting.

(7)

This blizzard kept us "snowed in" four days, and was pronounced by the Dodge City and Topeka papers the severest one ever known in the history of the State.

My business at Muscogee was to investigate another sale of lands by some of the Shawnee Indians, though not of Black Bob's band. In the course of this investigation I had to visit Vinita and the Sac and Fox Agency, in the Indian Territory, Chetopa and Oswego, Kansas, and Kansas City, Missouri.

Enroute to Sac and Fox I had to lay over a day at Red Fork, for want of transportation. Two old plainsmen who were getting ready to go hunting, invited me to accompany them. I was afterwards informed that they mistook me for a tenderfoot drummer, or "commercial pilgrim," as they expressed it, and expected to have some fun at my expense. They were exceedingly kind, however, and furnished me a good mount and gun.

Riding out in a northwesterly course we skirted the brakes of the Arkansas River up in the direction of the mouth of the Cimarron River. There was five inches of snow on the ground, just as there was at the time of my trip to Sac and Fox a year before. In some of the ravines it was twenty feet deep, and badly crusted. This made it difficult and somewhat dangerous to ride through the brakes, where bluffs and ravines were numerous.

Three or four miles out one of my companions got a long shot at a deer with a Winchester rifle. Finding blood, we set out on the trail   The blood soon ceased, and, our chase falling in with others, tracks became numerous.   Agreeing to meet in the afternoon at a certain high point which my companions pointed out to me, we separated, each taking a different trail.

My deer led me across a creek, and did not seem to be going anywhere in particular.   In fact he rather appeared to be just experimenting to see how crooked a trail he could make through the snow.   Finally I trailed him into the mouth of a shallow canyon.   Planning to head him off, I galloped along the ridge a few hundred yards towards the head of the canyon.   Then, in order to descend and approach with less noise, I dismounted some distance back from the bluff, tied my horse there, and started down on foot.

The brow of the bluff had been swept bare of snow by the winds.   From the brink there appeared to be a smooth slope to the broad bottom twenty-five feet below.   Starting down this declivity, at the very first step I failed to find footing.   Instead of being an incline, it was a perpendicular bluff twenty-five feet high.   The snow had simply blown over it and banked up from the bottom to the top.   Breaking through the crust, I fell headlong to the bottom, striking on some rough undergrowth and rocks, which stunned me to insensibility. My clothes were badly torn, and my face bruised and lacerated. Of course my fall was somewhat obstructed by the density of the snow; otherwise I certainly would have been killed outright.

When I regained consciousness I was almost frozen, snow having found its way down my collar, and up my sleeves, by the handful. My hat and gun were both missing. Feeling about in the snow, I at length found the gun, and then abandoning my hat, I tied a handkerchief around my head and groped my way out of the drift. This required exertions which so exhausted my strength that I thought I should succumb before I could struggle out. Having no idea of the right direction I did not go straight out. As I meandered, the distance was at least fifty yards.

Stopping to take a survey of myself, I was amazed at my wrecked condition. I could hardly have been worse battered up by a leap from the mythical "jumping off place" which is supposed to be the end of all reckless careers.

Limping along down the canyon to a place where the wall was less precipitous, I dragged myself up to the horse. My appearance was so changed that he not only failed to recognize me, but actually became frightened as I drew near. Rearing and plunging, he seemed about to break loose and leave me afoot there in the snow. As I was already in an exhausted condition, I felt sure that if he escaped from me I would perish before my comrades could track me up. But, by removing the handkerchief from my head, and approaching gently and coaxingly, I succeeded in quieting him. Getting hold of the bridle, I led him to a boulder, from which I managed to mount.

By this time my fondness for hunting seemed to be entirely extinguished. Anyhow I had enough of the sport for that day, and my intention was to ride straight to the designated meeting place, and there make a fire and await the arrival of my friends. I hoped that nothing would get in my way. I felt that the sight of game would be an annoyance to me. I did not wish to be troubled to even raise my gun and shoot. Badly hurt, cold, mad, tired and disgusted, I only wished that I could get back to Red Fork without moving again in my saddle.

But I had ridden less than three hundred yards when I was startled by a tremendous flapping of wings. A flock of turkeys being huddled together and sunning themselves in a bare spot on the south side of a boulder, I was in twenty feet of them before they arose to wing. Instantly my hurts and fatigue were forgotten, but before I could get my gun in hand all the turkeys were out of range, having separated and flown in various directions.   One very large gobbler apparently too heavy to fly far, alighted in a tree just beyond range. Seeing me riding towards him, he pitched off across a small creek.   When he was sixty yards from me, and perhaps forty feet above the earth, I fired, and he fell heavily in the snow.   Dismounting, I lifted him up against the side of the horse and tied him to the saddle.

Attempting to remount from the ground, I found myself too sore and stiff to accomplish that feat. Leading my horse and trudging some two hundred yards through the snow, I came to the trunk of a fallen tree, from which I remounted.

Being now utterly worn out it was still my wish to return to Red Fork without further trouble or delay. Of course I would shoot game if it got in my way. Nevertheless, I hoped that nothing would obtrude itself upon me.   But, as before, I had gone less than a quarter of a mile when my attention was arrested by a commotion in a clump of green briers on the bank of a small creek.   Halting to ascertain the cause, I was surprised to see that it was a deer—a beautiful young buck.   He was daintily browsing on the leaves of an evergreen vine.   Descrying me as I came to a halt, he bounded out of the thicket.   As he dashed away I gave him one barrel at a distance of perhaps eighty yards. Leaping high in the air, he came down on his back in the snow. Bounding to his feet again as quick as a flash, he sped furiously on eighty or ninety yards, and then fell dead. Tying him to the horn of the saddle with my picket-rope, I dragged him through the snow to the bank of a small ravine near by. Then leading my horse down into the ravine to a level with the bank, I rolled the deer across his back behind the saddle and tied it there with the saddle-strings.

Remounting with ease from the bank of the ravine, and riding slowly on down the margin of a small creek, I had proceeded not more than half a mile when a turkey flew from a tree a hundred yards in front, coming directly over me, and back in the direction from which I had just come. Turning in my saddle, I got the gun up when the turkey was about thirty feet from the ground and perhaps fifty yards directly in my rear. At the report of the gun he dropped in the snow just like a chunk, with both wings spread at full length.

This shot was also answered by a cheerful halloo from my friends, who happened to be just across a bend in the creek immediately in front of me. It was then clear that it was from them that the turkey had flown. As they came across I was much amused at the amazement with which they beheld the remarkable changes that had been wrought in my person and clothing since our separation less than four hours before.

"Hello, pilgrim; what you doin' with that hanker-cher on your head? Whur's your hat at?" one of them asked. Then as he drew nearer and got a better view of me, he exclaimed:

"Holy smoke! Been in a b'ar fight?"

"Sorry you sed b'ar fight!" his comrade remarked. "Lcoks more like he'd been blowed up with dinnimite! Say, pilgrim; how did you git killed, anyhow? And what in the name of Davey Crockett and Tom Walker tore them clothes offen you so scanless bad?"

"That's allus the way with a blamed tenderfoot; he allus thinks he can go anywhere and do anything any-body else can, and if you let him git out o' sight, he either kills his fool self or lets somethin' ketch him;" the first speaker went on to say in a tone that was delightfully hearty and cheerful in its mock derision.

Having heard my account of the accident, they dis-mounted and tied the turkey to my saddle to counter-balance the big gobbler I had previously killed. They also congratulated me upon my success, and one of them insisted that I should wear his hat back to Red Fork.

Their success had been greater than mine. They had two deer, three turkeys, and five mallard ducks, which, together with mine, was the largest amount of game I had seen killed in one day since my early boy-hood, when Arkansas was the huntsman's paradise.

Arriving at Red Fork an hour after dark, an hour later we were served with an excellent supper, including delicious venison steak from our own quarry.

Completing the investigation of the Shawnee land sale at Kansas City, I proceeded thence by way of Arkansas City, Kansas, to Osage Agency, in the Indian Territory, arriving there on the 7th of March.

CHAPTER XXIII.

PLACED IN CHARGE OF THE OSAGE AND KAW AGENCIES
—THE RICHEST PEOPLE IN THE WORLD—CHIEFS
BLACK DOG AND NECKAKAPAUNA—THE EMPLOYES.

INSPECTOR E. D. BANNISTER had been at Osage several days when I arrived there, and had already made a pretty thorough investigation. On the 9th of March he suspended the Agent from office, on the ground of incompetency and irregular conduct, and placed me in charge of the Agency.

Osage Agency is situated sixty-five miles southeast of Arkansas City, and thirty miles south of Cedar Vale, Kansas, in that part of the Indian Territory that has since been formed into Oklahoma Territory. There are only one thousand five hundred and sixty of the Osages, but they are said to be the richest tribe or nation of people in the world, in proportion to numbers. Their Reservation, which they bought from the Cherokees and paid for with their own money, contains one million four hundred and seventy thousand one hundred and ninety-six acres, which is nine hundred and forty-two acres for each person. The United States also holds in trust for them under treaty stipulations, $8,029,501.29 in actual cash, which is also theirs absolutely.

The annual interest on this vast sum is $401,475.06. Of this interest $250,000 is paid to them in quarterly payments of $40 per capita, that being as much as the Government considers that they need. The residue above $250,000, with the exception of a few thousand dollars used to defray the expenses of the Agency and the Reservation schools, accumulates in the United States treasury. This accumulated interest now amounts to more than a million dollars. But the Government pays no interest on it, and it is subject to distribution to the tribe at any time in the discretion of the Department.

Thus we see that the per capita share of each Indian in the common property of the tribe is nine hundred and forty-two acres of land and $5,787.14 in money. This gives to each family of five persons, and that is the average Indian family, four thousand seven hundred and ten acres, or upwards of seven square miles of land, and $28,935.70 in money. No civilized people on the globe have so large a per capita of either land or money, and no other tribe of Indians have as much money, though a few of them have more land.

It may be said that the Osages own this land and money in common, and that individually they own not an acre of the one nor a dollar of the other. In the abstract that is true. But each individual is allowed to take and occupy all the land he can make use of, and each member of the tribe draws an individual income from the money. As before stated, a part of the interest is paid to them every three months, the per capita of these quarterly payments being $40, or $160 per annum, the annual income of a family of five being $800, with a surplus accumulating in the treasury besides.

This is far better, of course, than if each individual or head of a family had possession or control of his particular share, for in that case the riches of many, like those of many white people, would soon take wings and fly away never to return.

And, in addition to this common property, many of the Osages are wealthy in their individual rights, in horses, cattle, improved farms, and other property. The Kaw Indians are also under the jurisdiction of the Agent at Osage. They are very poor in their individual rights, but in common property they also are rich. There are only one hundred and ninety-six of them, and their Reservation contains one hundred thousand one hundred and thirty-seven acres, which is

OSAGE SCHOOL.

five hundred and ten acres per capita, or two thousand five hundred and fifty acres, or four square miles, for each family of five persons. They also have $200,000 in the United States treasury, though a portion of the interest on that fund is used to defray the expenses of their Reservation school and Sub-Agency.

Both of these tribes live upon their own resources, the Government making no issues of rations or clothing to either of them. Most of them wear blankets, paint and feathers, and live in tents, but they are among the most tractable and easily governed Indians in the United States.

The Kaws still cling to their ancient tribal organization, but the Osages have a code of written laws, a legislative council and courts, and elect their chief, assistant chief, councilmen, judges, sheriffs, clerks and treasurers every two years by vote of all the male members of the tribe over the age of twenty-one years.

Black Dog, a stalwart and sagacious Indian, the son of an old-time chief, had been chief during the preceding term, but at the election held a few months previous to my arrival he was defeated by an old fellow named Neckakapauna.

Notwithstanding Black Dog's defeat for the office of chief, he was still the acknowledged leader of the Big Hills, a large band of full-bloods living on the Arkansas River some thirty miles from the Agency.

Neckakapauna was not only a plebeian, but his political opponents charged in the canvass for chief that he had no ancestry to speak of—that he was in fact a "scrub." Of course his partisans denounced that as a campaign lie, and it may have been. They not only admitted, but in their excess of democracy they were rather inclined to boast, that his parents were poor; but those who required proof that they were also respectable were left very much in doubt. But under their republican form of government the old commoner arose to the surface, triumphed over the royal house of Black Dog, and became chief of the tribe. He was a good Indian, however, and made a very good chief, his greatest disqualification for the position probably being his nonprogressiveness.

Osage Agency is a considerable village. In addition to the various Agency buildings, four large traders' stores are located there. Dwellings are furnished by the Government for all of the Agency employes who have families, and all of the traders and several of their clerks have comfortable private dwellings and keep their families there. A number of well-to-do half-breeds also live in the village.

I had no fault to find with any of the employes, except the two clerks. They were both notoriously incompetent and untrustworthy. I immediately requested the Department to send me two capable clerks in their places. Mr. James L. Gibson was promptly sent in the place of the assistant clerk, and I was well pleased with him. He was well qualified, and an honest, intelligent, well-bred young gentleman.

Mr. W. D. Wisdom, another young gentleman of high character and superior qualifications, was sent to me for a month, to help me get the affairs of the Agency out of the chaotic state in which I found them. But the Department probably considered that reform enough for one Agency, for at the end of the month Mr. Wisdom was ordered to Ponca Agency, and I was required to keep the little sawed-off chief clerk. It was evident to my mind that his relatives had procured this important place for him as an asylum from rum, and also because he was utterly worthless, incapable of making a living, and a source of social embarrassment at home. Having what the politicians and intriguers call a "pull" in Washington, they had probably procured his appointment, and held him in the place in spite of the protests of fast succeeding failing Agents, upon representations made like the darky recommended the 'possum dog:

"I ain' neber seed dat daug tree no 'possums," he said, "but den I know he *boun'* ter be a good 'possum daug, 'cause he ain' no 'count fur nuthin' else."

This clerk's salary was $1,200, but he was so hopelessly and stupidly incompetent that I and the assistant clerk, whose salary was only $1,000, had to do his work ourselves. I told him one day to write a letter transmitting a certain document to the Department. He bounced around as if he would dash it off in a second, bent over his desk and scribbled a minute or two, picked up a copy of the Department Regulations and searched through it in an exceedingly fidgety manner a few minutes, bent over his desk and scribbled some more, and finally brought me a scrawl which started off as follows:

"The Honored Commisionder of Indian Afairs, Washington, D. C.

DEAR SIRS:

Enclose herewith I handed you—"

I complimented him on that, of course, and told him that if he wanted to finish a day's work to get a blank and fill out a requisition on the "Honored Commisionder" for a "Blue Backed Speller" and a "Practical Letter Writer" for the use of the chief clerk, and I would sign it in capital letters. He laughed a little and said he "did not need *them* things, but he *would* like to have an adding machine and a lightning calculator, as he was not very good in figures."

At that time the Department appointed all of the

Agency clerks, and prohibited the Agents from select-
ing them, under the alleged doctrine that they might
choose persons with whom they could collude to perpe-
trate fraud. As all sensible men may imagine, the
result was that nearly every politician with a "pull"
was enabled to "unload" "a lame duck" on some
helpless Agent, often to his ruin, and always to the
injury and discredit of the service.

Dr. J. E. Dodson, of Texas, was physician; Perry
Primm, of Tennessee, general mechanic, and Andres
Nelson, of Iowa, superintendent of stock. They were
well suited to their respective places, and performed
their duties faithfully and intelligently throughout my
term.

Mr. Charles Fagan, of Indiana, was superintendent
of the Reservation school, and his wife, Mrs. Nettie
Fagan, Miss Mamie McCarthy, of Washington, D. C.,
and Miss Kate Miller, of Illinois, teachers. Mr. Fagan
was a very capable and successful superintendent, and
the teachers were well qualified for their places.

Mr. J. C. Keenan, of Indiana, was Sub-Agent and
superintendent of the school at Kaw. He was an
excellent man for the place, and managed the affairs of
that interesting little Agency so carefully and well that
they gave me no trouble whatever.

My predecessor was the Agent who had suffered the

Indians to camp around his house, to make a good impression on them, as described in a previous chapter; having proved entirely too weak for the place, as I had feared he would.   His predecessor had also failed through incompetency, and, as the reader may imagine, everything was badly demoralized.   The Reservation had become a green pasture for whisky peddlers, gamblers and horse thieves, an asylum for fugitives from justice, and a Garden of Eden for loafers.   These classes were almost as numerous as the Indians, and while the latter were not the least inclined to turbulency and insubordination, they were fast being demoralized and corrupted to absolute worthlessness and depravity.

The Indian police had become so badly demoralized that they could not be depended on for anything.   Two days before I was placed in charge, the Agent sent ten of them out to arrest two whisky peddlers.   But instead of submitting to arrest, the peddlers obtained a parley with the police, made the entire squad dead drunk, disarmed them and stampeded their ponies.

I reorganized the force from the best material in the tribe, but having no confidence even in them for the work then in hand, and being determined to rid the Reservation of all lawless characters, I reported the situation to the Department, and asked for a troop of cavalry.

CHAPTER XXIV.

A NOTABLE AND ROMANTIC INDIAN WEDDING—TWO
HANDSOME YOUNG SQUAWS AT ONCE—THE PECULIAR
POLYGAMOUS CUSTOM OF THE OSAGES—DANCING
AND HORSE RACING—HOW THEY MAKE THEIR BETS.

BLACK DOG and his entire band of Big Hill
Indians were encamped on the west side of Bird
Creek, about a mile from the Agency. They just
seemed to be out for a frolic, and were trading at the
stores, feasting, dancing, horse racing, and having what
they considered a good time generally.

Strike Axe's band was encamped near the race track,
which was situated a mile north of the Agency.   About
9 o'clock every morning Black Dog and his band
would come by on their way to the races.   All the
"race horse men" and many others being on horseback, and all the women, children and old men being
in covered hacks, wagons and buggies, they constituted
an irregular but exceedingly picturesque procession.

Many of their race horses are of American blood,

and really very fine animals. I remember one in particular, owned by Chief Strike Axe, that would have been considered a fine horse in any country.

They had an old-fashioned straight track on a level prairie, and their stakes were sometimes quite large. Like all other Indians they are fond of bunch races, and often fifteen and twenty came through under whip at once.

They have no judge at the starting point. The starter starts them as near even as possible, and the foremost one at the outcome is the winner and takes all the stakes. Two old "coffee coolers" sitting in the grass at the end of the track decide that question.

Their stakes are made up in very simple manner. Sometimes the stakeholder spreads a blanket on the grass, and calls for bets. The bettors deposit the stakes on the blanket, and name their horses. The stakes consist of silver coin and paper currency, pistols, Winchester rifles, belts, cartridges, blankets, shawls, moccasins, wampum, tobacco pouches, Sioux pipes, cigarettes, smoking tobacco, saddles, bridles, picket ropes, bands of sleigh bells, and various other articles of Indian property. Often, too, the stakeholder is seen holding the ropes of a considerable bunch of ponies, and now and then a hack or buggy may be seen drawn up near him.

At other times the stakeholder takes a light pole on his shoulder and goes through the camp calling for bets. The bettors hang their various stakes on the pole, and I have often seen it loaded until it took two to carry it.

The bettors on the winning horse take all the stakes, but how they divide them between themselves I never could understand. They have some way of doing it, however, which is well understood and entirely satisfactory, for I never heard of a quarrel growing out of a race during my stay at the Agency.

Early in May the most notable wedding ever known among the Osages occurred at an encampment a mile and a half north of the Agency.

I had heard of elaborate preparations being made for this wedding ever since my arrival, and one day in the latter part of April Neckakapauna, Strike Axe, and perhaps a dozen other head men, called on me at the office and invited me to attend it. Strike Axe had become a great friend of my wife, who was with me at that place, and he exacted a promise from me that I would take her also. He said he had always understood that "white squaws," like their Indian sisters, were fond of weddings, and as this was to be the grandest event of the kind in the history of the tribe, he wanted my "squaw" to see it.

Of course the whites expected that it would be an exceedingly novel wedding in all respects, but the thing most remarkable and interesting to them was that *the groom was to marry two squaws at once.* Although authorized by an old custom, such weddings are not frequent in the tribe, and the circumstances with which the Indians themselves were most delighted on this occasion were the great and unusual formalities of the ceremonies, and the gorgeousness and prodigality of the feast and celebration.

At 2 o'clock in the afternoon of the designated day, I drove out in a buggy with my wife to Strike Axe's camp. Two small creeks come together in the form of a V. Strike Axe's band, which for this occasion was swelled to the number of four hundred, was encamped on one of these creeks, and Neckakapauna, with a band of six hundred, was encamped on the other, the two encampments being about a quarter of a mile apart, with a beautiful valley, perfectly level and covered with luxuriant grass, extending entirely across from one to the other.

The father of the brides was a sub-chief or head man in Strike Axe's band, and the father of the groom was one of Neckakapauna's under chiefs. The large tents occupied by the families of Strike Axe and the father of the brides faced each other, and were situated in the center of the encampment.

For this occasion Strike Axe had induced me to loan him a large United States flag that belonged to the Agency, and the first thing to arrest our attention was this flag floating bottom edge up from the top of a wonderfully crooked, unpeeled hackberry pole about twenty feet high, propped up in the small space between his tent and that of the father of the brides.

All the tents were crowded very close together, but Strike Axe made way for us to drive up near this flag pole. Here we noticed a squaw holding two beautiful ponies that looked exactly alike. On their backs were great, soft, flat-topped pads, made of beautiful, high-priced blankets, and almost all the rest of their bodies were covered with beaded trappings, ribbons and sleigh bells.

In a few minutes squaws came and rolled up the front wall of the tent occupied by the girls. They were seated on a great carpet of buffalo robes and beautiful blankets of various colors and sizes. My wife and I both recognized them as two girls who had been at our house two or three times, and whom we had spoken of as making the nearest approach to real beauty of any full-bloods we had ever seen. They now looked really pretty, their costumes being by far the most beautiful of the kind that I have ever seen. They seemed to be about eighteen years old.

At a command from Strike Axe the girls both arose and came out to the ponies, each led by a handmaid. The squaw holding the ponies handed the handmaids a freshly peeled pole about the length and size of a hand-spike. The handmaids holding this pole within six inches of the ground by the side of one of the ponies, one of the girls stepped up on it, steadying herself by holding to the pad on the pony's back. The hand-maids then carefully raising the pole close up by the pony's side, the girl seated herself on the pad, sidewise; the entire feat being accomplished with consummate ease, grace and modesty. Turning then to the other girl, the handmaids assisted her to mount in the same way.

Everything now being ready, Strike Axe directed a stalwart young Indian to take the flag and head the procession to Neckakapauna's camp. Strike Axe and the father of the brides fell in immediately behind him, and then came the handmaids leading the two ponies side by side. They were followed by the mother and other relatives, and then came the entire band, regard-less alike of order and precedence.

Just as the head of the procession cleared the camp, Strike Axe fired a pistol as a signal to Neckakapauna, and instantly we saw a large crowd start to meet us. There was no road, and the procession moved in a slow walk right through the grass.   Pulling out some twenty steps to one side, I drove along about even with Strike Axe.

When the other crowd came out from their camp we saw that some of them were mounted and driving a bunch of ponies.   We also noticed eight squaws running ahead with two large blankets in their hands.   They were all coming much faster than we were traveling. But that was proper.   They were coming to meet the brides, and custom and gallantry alike required them to come with spirit and gladness.   To have gone mopingly would have been "bad form"—bad Osage form—very bad; whereas it was becoming to the brides to advance demurely.

When the eight squaws met us, they spread the blankets on the grass, and then locking their hands together, they lifted the girls off of the ponies and sat each of them down in the center of a blanket.   This, like the mounting, was very skillfully and beautifully done.

While this was going on the bridegroom's father was delivering the bunch of ponies to the brides' father. There were twenty of them and they were in payment for the girls.   The old man sending his herders hurrying back to his camp with the ponies, the squaws gathered up the blankets by the four corners and started on a run with them to the bridegroom's tent—it being a case of simultaneous payment and delivery of the goods.

The girls sat upright with their feet drawn up under them, but of course the blankets sagged down, and we could just see their heads as the squaws trotted along through the grass with them.

The bridegroom's tent was also a very large one, and set facing Neckakapauna's, in the first row of tents on the side fronting Strike Axe's camp, the walls being rolled up about six feet high all around. Several adjoining tents were also stretched so as to serve as awnings, and all were carpeted with buffalo robes and blankets. The bridegroom being seated alone on a great mat of blankets in his own tent, the squaws carried the two girls in without stopping, and sat one down on each side of him. They all looked about as confused and helpless as young white people usually do in the act of marriage, and if either of them uttered a word we failed to hear it.

The girls at once took off their jewelry, hats, and some of their outer garments, and, without rising, and with remarkable grace and dexterity, put on others which the bridegroom, also without rising, handed to them. This was symbolical of their renunciation of all dependence upon their father for raiment, and of the bridegroom's vow to supply their necessities in that respect.

Squaws then brought in a double-width of oilcloth about thirty feet long, and spread it on the blankets and robes immediately in front of the brides and groom. Other squaws placed plates and other dishes around the edges, and brought in various articles of cooked food in large pans and bowls.

The brides and groom were given just one plate, one cup, and one small dish of each article of food. It was now nearly 4 o'clock, and when all was ready the feast began, the chiefs of both bands, and members of the families of the high contracting parties sitting down to the oilcloth, and the rest of the two bands dividing up into small groups under the various tents and awnings throughout the camp.

The brides and groom ate from the same dishes, he taking the first mouthful from each dish and then handing it first to the girl at his right hand and then to the one at his left hand. He took the first sup of coffee, and then handed the cup to each of the girls in turn. They ate but little, but whatever it was it constituted a part of the ceremony, and when the feast ended the marriage was complete.

It is proper to say here that the Government discountenances polygamy among the Indians, and Agents are instructed to break up the practice wherever it can be done without results equally detrimental to the Indians, or hazardous to the whites, and I would have prevented this marriage if I had been a permanent Agent. But as polygamy had not been arbitrarily prohibited by my predecessors, and probably would not be by my successor, it was obvious that it would do more harm than good to interfere in this particular case.

The polygamous custom of the Osages is a peculiar one. An Osage may marry two squaws at once, and perhaps even more, or take a plural wife or wives at any time, but if all of the women die, or desert him, or he abandons them or either of them, he is never allowed to marry again. That is the penalty that the unwritten law of the tribe lays upon him for taking more than one man's share of the women at once. If both of these girls had died or deserted the young fellow in an hour he never would have been permitted to marry again. This law is inexorable.

CHAPTER XXV.

A PICTURESQUE COUNTRY—WHISKY PEDDLERS AND
OKLAHOMA BOOMERS—A VISIT FROM THE KAWS—
ORIGIN OF THE NAMES OF THE STATES OF ARKANSAS
AND KANSAS.

THE Osage Reservation is a picturesque country.
The uplands are high and rolling, and the valleys
broad and fertile. Building stone is abundant, and
there are innumerable streams fringed with timber.
Many of the streams are of living water, and swarm
with fish, the bass being particularly numerous. During the spring I found time to go fishing occasionally,
though in addition to the usual duties of Agent I had
to devote a great deal of time to whisky peddlers and
"Oklahoma boomers."

And the Agent who has to deal with those two
classes of trespassers needs an unusual amount of recreation. They were both very troublesome on the Osage
Reservation, but with the aid of the Indians I held my
hand with them quite successfully. It was my rule at

all the Agencies I was ever in charge of to have the Indians do the most of that kind of work themselves. My first experience in that line at Osage was quite amusing.   The Indians wanted to have a big dance and feast.   I withheld my consent until the chiefs promised me that if any whisky peddlers came about they would arrest them and turn them over to me.

About 4 o'clock in the afternoon of the first day of the dance four head men came galloping up to my yard gate and called to me in broken English:

"Whisky peddlers! Two! Indians ketch him.   Tie him. You come and see him, now. Neckakapauna and Strike Axe say so."

Going with them, they carried me through the center of the camp, which was situated in a valley a mile and a half from the Agency, and as I passed along every Indian in sight gave me an unusually friendly greeting.

On the bank of the little creek about a quarter of a mile above the camp, and near the edge of a dense thicket, we found all the chiefs and head men sitting in a circle around the two whisky peddlers, who were stretched out on their backs, and so securely bound with ropes that they could move neither hand nor foot. There must have been fifty feet of rope wound and tied around each of them, and they could just barely move their heads.   They were excellent specimens of their class—resolute, desperate and "tough"—and their capture had only served to make them stubborn and spiteful.

The Indians were greatly elated over their achievement, and the chiefs and head men took extreme delight in showing me the peddlers' "outfit," which consisted of a buggy and span of ponies, two Winchester rifles, four pistols, and half a bushel of cartridges; two five-gallon kegs and six one-gallon jugs, all full of a very bad quality of whisky, except one of the kegs, from which they had been selling, and which was only about half full.

With this "outfit" they had established themselves in the thicket about noon, and immediately commenced a cautious but lively business. Six one-gallon jugs had gone for six ponies worth $40 apiece, and half the contents of one of the kegs had been retailed out at $10 per quart.

All my readers may not understand why Indians will pay such exorbitant prices. It is because the sale of intoxicating liquor to them, or the introduction of it into their country, is punishable under the laws of the United States by heavy fine and imprisonment in the penitentiary, for which reason white men will not take the risk of selling to them without outlaw profits.

When I asked these peddlers some questions concerning themselves they refused to answer, and after swearing at me for some time with marvelous strength and fluency, asked me in turn what I intended to do with them. That being an opportunity to get "even" which I could not resist, I "comforted" them with the information that I had decided to let the Indians haul them down into Bird Creek bottom and kill them.

I had already told Neckakapauna to send some young men with a wagon to haul them to the guardhouse, my intention being to hold them for the U. S. Marshal. When the wagon came they were hastily thrown in, and the driver started back through the camp at a brisk trot. The road was strewn with large cobblestones, and as I fell in behind I noticed that the prisoners were being unmercifully jolted, bouncing sometimes like blocks of wood clear to the top of the wagon box. Unheeding this cruelty, and with manifest enjoyment of the yelling and terrible execrations of the prisoners, the driver was plying his whip with increased, rather than diminished, vigor, and I had to send a mounted Indian at full-speed to make him "slow down."

As I was passing through the camp I came very near riding over an Indian who was lying on the grass, bound hand and foot, just like the peddlers. I called the chiefs and asked what it meant. They answered: "Heap drunk. All time heap holler. Injuns tie him,

(8)

too." Then they carried me around to different places and showed me seven others whom they had disposed of in the same way. It was the intoxication of those Indians that gave the chiefs notice of the presence of the peddlers.

But the morning sun rose on an empty guardhouse. During the night confederates of the prisoners cut down the heavy door and liberated them. Upon learning that, I destroyed the whisky and confiscated the remainder of the "outfit" to the captors.

Prior to this circumstance I had two or three times found it necessary to lead the police in person against these outlaws, but afterwards whenever I heard of whisky peddlers or invading boomers, all I had to do was to let the chiefs know that I wanted them. By that means I had pretty effectually cleared the Reservation of such characters before the troop of cavalry arrived.

Some of the boomer outfits of that day were almost as hard and dangerous to deal with as the whisky peddlers. Boomers are people who invade Indian country and try to take possession of it before it is opened by law for white settlement. Many of them have wagon beds almost as large as box cars, with roof, stove and sleeping berths, and actually live on wheels. They generally go in crowds of from two to ten families, and sometimes have considerable herds of horses and cattle. At that time hundreds of them were trying to invade the country then known as Oklahoma through the Osage and Ponca Reservations, which lay between that country and Kansas. I and Agent Osborne, of Ponca, had orders to guard all the roads on our Reservations, and turn these boomers back.

One morning while Osborne was at breakfast word was brought to him that a large crowd were coming down the road right through his Agency. He rushed out to his yard gate to turn them back, as he was ordered to do. As they came up he asked one of them where they were going. The boomer jerked a double-barreled shot gun out of a wagon, cocked both barrels in Osborne's face, gritted his teeth, and exclaimed:

"*Oak-lay-homey!*——*!!*——*!!! Oak-lay-homey!!!!*"

Osborne had the reputation of being the bravest Agent and the greatest wag in the service. At this instant his sense of the ridiculous overcame him. Bowing with excessive politeness to the boomer, he said in a half-comical, half-confidential tone:

"My dear friend, that is a magnificent country down there, and I am one of its authorized immigration agents. This is a direct road to it. Drive right ahead, and if anybody attempts to stop you, just send for me!"

The next day he overtook them with a band of In-

dians and brought them all back—he and the shot gun
man, whose name also happened to be Osborne, claiming, in the most ridiculous mock affection, to be
"cousins."

One day at Osage I had to call out the entire police
force and several volunteer Indians to turn back a party
composed of nine men and seven women. The women
had guns in their hands and for a time looked even
more desperate and dangerous than the men; but,
women like, they weakened and called for quarter when
they saw their "men folks" in danger.

About the first of June Mr. Keenan reported that the
Kaws had their crops nicely "laid by"—finished—and
wanted permission to visit the Osages. I granted their
request, and when they arrived all the chiefs and head
men called on me at the office to thank me, and to say
that they would stay seven days.

There is a Government ice house at Osage, and in
the winter the Agency and school employes combine
and fill it with ice for their own use during the summer.

Four days after the arrival of the Kaws the chiefs
and head men returned to the office looking so sad and
dejected that I was afraid they had met with some great
calamity. They said they were very much troubled,
and wanted to talk with me. I told them that it grieved
me to see them in distress, and that if I could do any-

thing to make them happy it would give me happiness to do it.

That cheered them up wonderfully, and Washunga, the principal chief, said I was a good Agent, just like Major Laban J. Miles, who had been their Agent for several years, and that as the favor they had come to ask of me was easily within my power, they had felt sure from the start that I would grant it, just as they knew Major Miles would do if he were Agent. Of course that touched my vanity a little, as it was ingeniously intended to do, and with another assurance of my kindly disposition towards them, I told Washunga to make their wishes known without further ado. Rising and drawing his sheet closely around him, he shook hands with me and proceeded in the most formal and ceremonious manner as follows:

"Washunga's people have all worked very hard this year, and are very tired. They have made no visit to any of their friends, and have had no play. They have good crops. They have worked them well and laid them by. Washunga's people are not lazy. Mr. Keenan says they have done well. Four sleeps ago we came here to visit our friends, the Osages. They are rich and have plenty to eat, and many presents to give us. We have been feasting and dancing and having a happy time. We want to stay and dance three days

longer. But last night my friend's pappoose died—
squaw pappoose, six snows old. My friend is a good
man. This is him here—pointing to a head man at his
side. He does not want to bury his pappoose here in
the Osage country. He wants to take it back and bury
it in our own country. But the weather is very warm,
and he cannot keep his pappoose three days in the
camp. It would keep that long in your ice house, and
he wants to put it in there until he dances three more
days, and then he will take it home and bury it! That
is what we have come to ask our good, kind Agent to
let him do!''

Instead of recovering from the immediate shock of
this gruesome request, it grew on me until finally I had
to forego the use of ice water entirely for nearly two
years. For a long time I could not take a drink of it
without seeing Washunga and his friend and the dead
pappoose at the bottom of the glass.

Of course I made the Indian take his pappoose home
and bury it that day, and gave him the best lecture I
could on the better instincts of humanity, but I had not
the heart to speak harshly to him. He moved me to
pity and not to anger. I could not forget that he was
only a benighted savage, really well disposed, and
utterly incapable of realizing the brutality of his conduct.

It was from this tribe that the State of Kansas derived

its name. It was originally spelled, and the Indians themselves still pronounce it, Konza. Catlin, who visited the tribe in 1830, and who is universally recognized authority on Indian nomenclature, spelled it that way, both in his book and on his maps. Kaw and Kansas are both corruptions of the name, and the latter, I think, an extremely harsh one. And worst of all, to sound the terminal s is to make it the plural of the name. Catlin spells it, singular, Konza; plural, Konzas.

This name also forms a part of the name of the State of Arkansas, which is correctly pronounced as if spelled Arkansaw, the terminal letter s being silent. The early French explorers called the Arkansas River the River of the Arc, on account of the arc which it describes in its sweep from its source to its mouth. The lower part of the Great Smoky Hill River was known in that region as the River of the Konzas, and the early settlers on the Lower Arkansas got the two rivers confused. They thought the Great Smoky Hill was known by that name all the way to its mouth, and that the Upper Arkansas was the River of the Konzas. This was a natural mistake in that day of limited geographical knowledge, because the two rivers at one point in Kansas approach very near to each other, and the Konzas roamed the valleys of both alike.

So in the course of time, either by design or formulative process of pronunciation, the two names of what was supposed to be the same river—Arc and Konza—were blended into the one beautiful name—Arkansas—the Kansas orthography of the latter in the plural number, and the soft, Indian pronunciation of it in the singular number, being adopted. Indeed, when you hyphenate these two names, Arc-Konza, or pronounce them together, Arc and Konza, you perceive that they blend themselves.

CHAPTER XXVI

RELIEVED AT OSAGE—INSPECTION OF VARIOUS AGEN-
CIES—PLACED IN CHARGE OF THE KIOWA, COMANCHE
AND WICHITA AGENCY.

ABOUT the first of June Captain Carroll H. Potter, of the Army, who had been detailed to relieve me of the charge of Osage Agency, arrived there for that purpose. The next day Captain A. E. Woodson came in from Fort Reno with his troop of cavalry, in compliance with the request that I had made for troops on taking charge of the Agency in March. A few days later the wives of those officers also arrived, and during the month of June they and my family experienced the discomforts and privations of the place in the same house.

Transferring the Agency to Captain Potter on the first of July, I first carried my family home, and then immediately departed on a tour of inspection, which included the Ponca, Pawnee, Otoe and Oakland, the Sac and Fox, the Cheyenne and Arapahoe, and the Kiowa, Comanche and Wichita Agencies.

RESERVATION SCHOOL, PONCA AGENCY.

The first four of these Agencies are situated in a group on the south side of the Arkansas River, and immediately west of the Osage Reservation.   The three latter are Sub-Agencies of Ponca, whose Agent at that time was Major E. C. Osborne, of Tennessee.

Major Osborne was a good Agent, and having two of the very best clerks in the service, Mr. W. D. Wisdom, who had been with me a month at Osage, and Mr. H. L. Douglass, of Nashville, Tennessee, of course all the affairs of his Agency were in excellent order. Major Osborne was especially proud of the Tonkawas— the Indians of the Oakland Agency—and the Pawnees; and he certainly had cause to be, for at that time both tribes were showing encouraging signs of improvement, especially in practical farming.   Mr. M. L. McKenzie as clerk was in immediate charge of Pawnee Agency, and doubtless was entitled to much of the credit for the progress of that tribe.

The Tonkawas used to be cannibals, and at one time the tribe was large and powerful.   But their numbers had been greatly decimated in wars with other tribes, and finally, in 1862, the Comanches suddenly fell upon them one day and massacred them all, except one small band which happened to be absent on a buffalo hunt. The survivors now number but sixty-eight persons.

I was occupied ten days in the inspection of those

Agencies, and then proceeded from Pawnee to Sac and Fox, where I had an extremely mean and troublesome Chicago drummer to deal with. He had abandoned his wife and children at Glens Falls, New York, and taken up with a half-breed widow of advanced age, who was the owner of property, and entitled to tribal rights, which I think he coveted more than he did her. The Agent promptly expelled him from the Reservation, but being a talented penman, he immediately opened up an amazingly voluminous and breezy correspondence with the Department. As a letter writer the Agent was no match for him at all. In fact in that line, as in various others, he was really an "artist" of astonishing ability. Notwithstanding he was a flagrant intruder, a fomenter of disturbance and discord among both whites and Indians, and altogether undeserving of any official indulgence, he soon argued, bluffed or hoodooed the Department into issuing a peremptory order to the Agent to allow him to return to the widow's until a Special Agent could get around there to investigate the case; and when I arrived he was just about to take possession of the Agency and expel the Agent. Of course my report was adverse to him, and vindicatory of the Agent.

From Sac and Fox I returned by way of Pawnee and Otoe to Ponca, and proceeded thence by way of Okla-

A CHEYENNE CAMP.

homa Station, on the Santa Fe Railroad, to the Cheyenne and Arapahoe Agency.

That being before the opening of Oklahoma to white settlement, where the City of Oklahoma now stands there was nothing but a small railroad station house, a water tank, and a miserable stage station.

I stopped a week at the Cheyenne and Arapahoe Agency, and then went on down to the Kiowa, Comanche and Wichita Agency, arriving there on the 26th of August.

Charges of dishonesty, drunkenness, and various other acts of misconduct, had been preferred against the Agent, and I had orders to make a careful investigation. I soon had abundant ocular proof of the second allegation. My arrival was about the middle of a Sunday afternoon, and before night five different employes came about the boarding house so drunk they could hardly walk. Having heard of my arrival, every one, drunk man like, made ridiculous efforts to "play sober," and seemed extremely desirous of making my acquaintance and assuring me that the Agent was the "best man that ever was," and that all the affairs of his Agency were in perfect order. Calling on the Agent at his residence after supper, I found him in the same condition as the employes.

It took me two months and a half to complete the

investigation, my report being submitted on the 8th of October. My findings were that the Agent had been habitually in a state of intoxication; that he had converted public funds to his own use; that he had presented false accounts and forged vouchers against the Government; that he had misapplied public property; that he had been in collusion with the beef contractor to swindle in the weights and quality of beef; that he had leased a portion of his Reservation to cattlemen for grazing purposes contrary alike to the wishes of the Indians and the instructions of the Department; that he had converted to his own use large sums of money paid to him by cattlemen for grazing lands on the Reservation; that he had suffered habitual drunkenness among his employes; that he was often unnecessarily absent from his Agency without leave; and that his habits were so irregular, and his official course so capricious and tyrannical, that he worried and dissatisfied the Indians and provoked them to resentment and mutiny.

As soon as my report was received in Washington the Agent was removed from office and I was ordered to take charge of the Agency, which I did on the 19th of October.

This is one of the largest and most important Agencies in the United States, and in many respects, I think, the most interesting of all. It embraces two separate Reservations, and nine different tribes, the population being as follows: One thousand six hundred and twenty-four Comanches, one thousand one hundred and fifty-one Kiowas, three hundred and twenty-five Apaches, five hundred and forty-five Caddoes, one hundred and seventy-five Wichitas, one hundred and fifty Tehuacanas, ninety-five Delawares, thirty-five Wacoes, and sixty-six Keechis—four thousand one hundred and sixty-six in all. These Indians speak nine different languages or distinct dialects, and have as many different distinguishing tribal characteristics.

The Agency is situated on the south bank of the Washita River, which separates the two Reservations. The name of the post office is Anadarko—the beautiful name of a tribe that once also belonged to the Agency, but is now extinct.

The Wichitas, Caddoes, Tehuacanas, Delawares, Wacoes and Keechis all live on the Wichita Reservation, which lies on the north side of the Washita, and contains about seven hundred and fifty thousand acres. The Wichitas are the original occupants of this country, and they have always been friendly towards the whites. It is their boast that they have never raised a hostile hand against a white man, and that they have always been loyal and obedient to the Government.

Most of the Caddoes, Delawares, Tehuacanas and Wacoes have log houses, but a great many of them

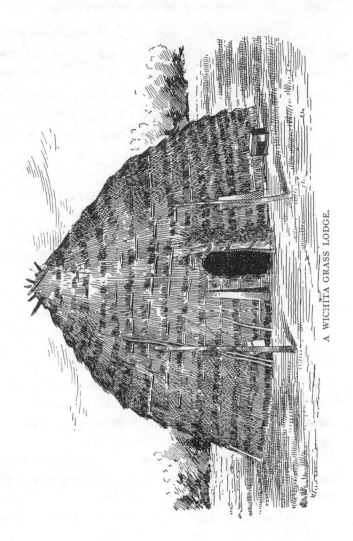

A WICHITA GRASS LODGE.

dwell in tents. The Wichitas also have some log houses, but a large majority of them still inhabit their famous grass lodges—lodges which are in form and structure peculiar to the Wichitas, and altogether unlike the lodges of any other Indians in the United States.

Of these affiliated bands the Caddoes are the most advanced in enlightenment and civilization. They are capable of self-support, and all the women, and most of the men, wear civilized dress. They, and also all the other affiliated Indians, own farms individually, or in communities, and produce some good crops. They also own a great many horses, cattle, hogs, wagons and other property.

The "wild tribes" of the Agency are the Comanches, Kiowas and Apaches. As late as 1876 these three tribes were the terrors of the plains and frontier settlements from Nebraska to the Gulf of Mexico, and from the Arkansas River to the Pecos and the Rio Grande. They now reside peaceably on their own Reservation, and many of them, especially of the Comanches, are making encouraging progress towards self-support in civilized pursuits.

Their Reservation contains nearly three million acres, being about sixty-five miles square, and it is one of the richest and most beautiful countries that I have ever seen. It is situated in the southwest corner of Oklahoma, adjoining Texas.

CHAPTER XXVII.

DESCRIPTION OF AN ISSUE OF BEEF CATTLE—HOW
RATIONS ARE ISSUED FROM THE WAREHOUSE—A
"HEAP BIG HOSS RACE."

R EGULAR bi-weekly issues of rations are made at
Anadarko to all the Indians on both Reservations, the aggregate quantities of the principal articles
issued during the year that I was in charge being three
million five hundred thousand pounds of beef, and six
hundred thousand pounds of flour.

For bi-weekly issues the Agent is first required to
divide the year's supply of each article into twenty-six
equal parts, which gives him one part for each issue in
the year.   One part is then divided by the whole number of Indians on the Reservation, and that gives the
ration of each Indian at each issue.

Once a year an actual count of all the Indians is
made, and the census roll of each band corrected by
subtracting the deaths and adding the births.   This is
a piece of work that requires great care and watchful-

ness, for many of these once guileless children of the prairies are now civilized to the degree that they are not too truthful to deny deaths, nor too honest to pass their pappooses around to be exhibited for enrollment by different families.

Upon the completion of the census a ticket is made out for each head of a family, showing his name, the name of his band, his number on the census roll, the number of persons in his family, the total number of rations that they are entitled to receive at each issue, and the dates of the issues. As the squaws draw all the rations except the beef, these tickets are turned over to them, and they carry them in little rawhide cases which they make themselves for the purpose.

Before the hour arrives for the issue the supplies are first weighed in bulk and then trucked to the counters and opened, so as to be convenient for weighing and measuring by the family ration. The squaws are admitted in line at one door, and pass out at another. The issue clerk is stationed with the interpreter near the entrance. When a squaw presents her ticket to him he punches out the date and calls the number of rations. She hands her sacks across the counter, and one employe gives her flour, another sugar and salt, another beans and rice, and another soap and baking powder.

In this way issues can be made with accuracy to sev-

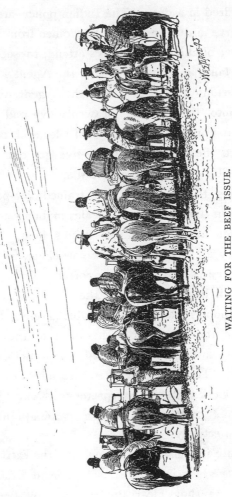

WAITING FOR THE BEEF ISSUE.

eral hundred in a day.   The Indian police are required
to preserve order and keep the women from crowding.
A number of chiefs also always attend, to see that the
issue is fairly made, and to sign the Agent's vouchers.

For issuing the beef cattle the Agent divides the
Indians into "beef bands" of twenty-five and fifty persons, and appoints a "beef chief" for each band.   At
Anadarko the bands of twenty-five get one beef, and
those of fifty get two, at each issue.

Entering the corral on their trained cow-ponies, the
herders run the cattle on the scales in bunches of from
two to ten head, and a clerk weighs them.   From the
scales they are turned into a narrow chute, which opens
on the prairie outside of the corral.   There they are
given fresh hair-brands with the Government irons, so
that the Indians may have no trouble in selling the hides.

All the Indians are present, most of the men and
boys being armed and mounted, to participate in the
slaughter.   The cattle being where all can see them,
the issue clerk with the interpreter calls out the names
of the chiefs, and points out the cattle apportioned to
them, respectively.

The gate is then thrown open, and the cattle, smart-
ing from the branding irons, make a mad dash for the
prairie.   As they clear the chute, from two to ten
mounted Indians fall in behind each one and open fire

on it, some with revolvers and some with Winchester rifles.

It usually takes three hours to complete the issue—the average turn-out being one per minute—and from the beginning to the end painted and feathered Indians and infuriated long-horned Texas steers are running in every direction for a mile around.   The marksmanship of the Indians is surprisingly bad—an average of five shots to the animal, or a thousand in all, being required to complete the slaughter, the number of cattle being two hundred.   They are struck in every part of the body from the hoofs to the horns.

The squaws being near at hand with the wagons and hacks, as soon as an animal falls they gather around it with their knives and begin skinning and dividing. The men assist some in this work, though the women do the most of it.   Fires are also made and very soon cooking and eating is going on throughout the camps.

The beef is cut into thin slices or strips and hung in the sun and over the fires to dry.   By the next day it is well cured, and then most of the Indians load up their pack-ponies and wagons and return to their permanent camps.

At the third issue after I took charge the Indians gave me an extremely painful scare, causing me to think for about one minute that five minutes would probably

AT THE BEEF ISSUE.

terminate my life.   Nobody knew anything about it at the time, however, and after it was all over I considered it a capital joke on myself.

Through the center of the widely scattered, rambling Agency village, there is a broad, smooth road, which the Indians had always used as a race-track.   As there had been no rain for several months, every time a race was run a great cloud of dust went rolling into the houses.   Besides that, there were quite a number of children at the Agency, and they, and even grown people, both white and Indian, were liable to be run over. So without consulting anybody, I posted an order in writing forbidding any more racing there after the second issue-day.   When that became known nearly all the employes and traders told me that I had attempted a reform that could not be accomplished.   They said they were sure the Indians would not obey the order, and that I could not make them do it.

I told the chiefs that I had no objection to their racing anywhere else, and would even send the Indian employes and police with tools to assist in laying out another track just back of the Agency.   Nevertheless, their faces showed great dissatisfaction, and as they dropped no intimation as to what they proposed to do about it, I became somewhat apprehensive that the opinion of the employes might be correct.   This apprehension was most troublesome in the reflection that as I was only temporarily in charge I could have ignored the nuisance just as well as not.

About 3 o'clock in the afternoon of the third issue-day, Mr. J. W. Carson, the chief of the Agency police, reported that an unusually large crowd of Comanches, Kiowas, Caddoes and Apaches had assembled at each end of the track and were running races, as he expressed it, "to beat the devil."

I told him to order them to stop it, and if they did not obey, to arrest the transgressors and bring them to the office. He departed without a word, but the expression on his face was about such as might have been expected if he had been ordered to stand on the railroad track and knock the lightning express off with a club.

Although the order could just as well have been omitted, it was a proper one, and since it had been published its enforcement was absolutely necessary to the maintenance of my authority as Agent; and while I did not tell Mr. Carson so, it was my intention for him to make the attempt, and if he failed, to telegraph to Fort Sill for troops. If the rule was unjust, I could afterwards revoke it with good effect, but at that stage of the proceedings I could not recede from it without loss of respect.

In a short while Carson galloped back with the report that the Indians claimed to have understood that the order was not to take effect until the next issue-day. They said the reason so many had assembled was that they understood it to be the last day on the old track, and all wanted to run a sort of farewell race.   Carson said the traders had also misunderstood the day, and had donated twenty dollars worth of provisions to be distributed as prizes on four bunch races.   He reported also that the chiefs were entirely reasonable and would desist at once if I insisted on it, but in view of the mis-understanding, and especially as that was a better track than the new one, they hoped I would at least suffer them to run the four prize races there.

Of course, under the circumstances, this request could not be denied, and as those four races were to be rather extraordinary, as well as the last on the old track, I concluded to go up from the office to the Agent's house and witness them myself. The Agent's dwelling, a two-story brick cottage, is situated a hundred yards back from the track, near midway its length, and com-mands an unobstructed view of it from one end to the other.   I was the sole occupant of the house at the time, and going out on the upper porch, I sat down alone.

There were eight ponies in the first race, seven in the second, and, I thought, thirteen in the third.

INDIANS WATERING THEIR PONIES AT A WELL.

After the third race all the Indians at the upper end of the track rode back and joined the big crowd at the starting point. A long parley ensued, and as they kept crowding closer together on their ponies and talking excitedly, I began to wonder what it meant. Looking through a spyglass I tried to see what Carson was doing, but as he had retired to a shade and dismounted, I could not find him. And there was no other white person in sight. All the employes were off at their duties, and as the stores were thronged with squaws and other Indians the traders and clerks were all indoors and taking no notice of what was going on outside.

Finally Quanah Parker, the chief of the Comanches, rode out in front of the crowd and began to speak. I could see that his remarks were being received with many demonstrations of approval, and in a few minutes he commenced riding back and forth, apparently forming the crowd into a straight front across the street, which at that place is perhaps fifty yards wide. There seemed to be about ten lines of them extending entirely across from Erwin's boarding house to Reynolds' store. These maneuvers were so unusual that the wonder with which I viewed them was no longer unmixed with apprehension.

Being mounted on a large iron-grey American horse,

Quanah Parker was a very commanding figure. When he seemed to get all the lines formed to his satisfaction, he rode to the center of the street, faced the crowd, took off his hat, spoke a few words, and then galloped to one side. Wheeling there and facing the crowd again, he drew his six-shooter and fired it off in the air.

Then came my panic! The pistol was the signal to "go," and the whole crowd "went"——went like a hurricane——every one yelling and quirting his pony as if his life depended on the effort.

The thought seized me that they had concluded not to submit to the order, and were coming to dispose of me right then and there. With the quickly formed determination to get at least one shot at them as they came over the yard fence, I ran into my room and jerked up a Winchester rifle. But as I got back to the porch the whole crowd was sweeping up the track like a cyclone, not one looking to the right or the left, but all still yelling and quirting their ponies with undiminished energy.

Just then I saw Carson come loping around from behind the great cloud of dust. Dismounting at the gate, he laughed and asked me if it was not the biggest horse race I ever saw. To my inquiry as to what it meant, he said that fifteen ponies were to have been entered in the last race, but when the time came all wanted to be in it, and not enough of them would submit to being ruled out to bring the number down even as low as fifty. Finally Quanah Parker proposed that as it was the last race on the old track, they give back the prize, and all run through and get all the fun they could out of it.

In fifteen or twenty minutes the entire crowd came riding back on their way to the new track, all laughing, talking and teasing one another. As they passed immediately in front of the house every one saluted me in some friendly manner, and several of them said:

"Heap big hoss race! Go to it now, the new track. Cut it off, the old track. All right. You say so."

Carson failed to notice that I had been in a panic, or was too respectful and polite to appear to have noticed it, and it was a long time before I told the joke on myself.

CHAPTER XXVIII.

THE COMANCHES—QUANAH, THE NOTED CHIEF—CYN-
THIA ANN PARKER, THE WHITE CAPTIVE—THRILLING
NARRATIVES BY GENERAL ALFORD AND GOVERNOR
ROSS.

CREDIT was conceded to the Comanches, and
mainly to Quanah, the chief of that tribe, for the
cheerful obedience of the Indians to the order relating
to horse-racing at Anadarko.

As a rule the most obedient, self-reliant and trustworthy Indians of the present day are those that were
in the days of the war-trail the bravest and most in-
domitable warriors. This is notably true of the
Comanches. Before their subjugation they surpassed
all the plains Indians in enterprise and daring being
the scourge of all the frontier settlements from the Arkansas to the Rio Grande. But since 1876 they have
lived peaceably on their Reservation and been uncom-
plainingly submissive to the authority of the Agent.

Much credit for the present good character of this

famous tribe is unquestionably due to Quanah Parker, the principal chief, who in the old days was himself a redoubtable warrior.

This distinguished chief has an exceedingly romantic and interesting history, being a son of the noted chief, Petanocona, and the unhappy white captive, Cynthia Ann Parker.

Desiring to give the readers of this narrative the pathetic story of the life of this sorrow-burdened captive in connection with that of her famous barbarian son, I wrote to Governor Ross for an account of her capture by the Indians, and recapture and restoration to her kindred by himself, and received the following polite and thoughtful answer:

EXECUTIVE OFFICE, AUSTIN, June 7th.

DEAR SIR—I have recently written a full account of the rescue of Cynthia Ann Parker and Lizzie Ross, at the request of General Geo. F. Alford, of Dallas. I am too much occupied with public matters to go over it again, but if you will address General Alford I am sure he will supply you a copy. Thanking you for your kindly expressions in regard to the matter, I am,

Yours respectfully,

L. S. ROSS.

Acting upon Governor Ross' suggestion, I then wrote to General Alford, and received the following courteous reply from him:

(9)

DALLAS, TEXAS, June 11th.

MY DEAR SIR—I have your favor of the 9th inst., requesting a copy of Governor Ross' letter to me in regard to the recapture of Cynthia Ann Parker. The document was written to give me data from which to write a historical sketch of this most important part of Texas history. I hope to have the article ready for the July number of "The Round Table," a literary periodical published in this city. When published I will take pleasure in mailing you a copy.

Sincerely yours,

GEO. F. ALFORD.

In due time I also received the promised copy of *The Round Table* containing General Alford's article, "Early Life in the Lone Star Republic," from which I extract the following graphic accounts relating to "The White Comanche:"

"Amongst numerous illustrations of heroism which illumine the pages of Texas history perhaps none shines with a brighter halo than the capture of Fort Parker.

In 1833 a small colony formed in Illinois, moved to the then Mexican province of Texas, and settled in a beautiful and fertile region on the Navasota River, about two miles from the present City of Groesbeck, the county seat of Limestone County. The colony consisted of nine families, in all thirty-four persons, of which Elder John Parker was the patriarchal head. They erected a blockhouse, which was known as Fort Parker, for protection against the assaults of hostile Indians. This structure was made of solid logs, closely knit together and hewn down so as to make a compact, perfect square, without opening of any kind until it reached a height of ten or twelve feet, where the structure widened on each side, forming a projection impossible to climb. The lower story, reached only by an interior ladder, was used as a place of storage for provisions. The upper story was divided into two large rooms with portholes for the use of guns, which rooms were used as living rooms and reached only by a ladder from the outside which was pulled up at night, after the occupants had ascended, making a safe fortification against any reasonable force unless assailed by fire.

These hardy sons of toil tilled their adjacent fields by day, always taking their arms with them, and retired to the fort at night. Success crowned their labors and they were prosperous and happy. On the morning of May 18, 1836, the men, unconscious of impending danger, left as usual for their fields, a mile distant. Scarcely had they left the inclosure when the fort was attacked by about seven hundred Comanches and Kiowas, who were waiting in ambush. A gallant and most resolute defense was made, many savages being sent by swift bullets to their "happy hunting grounds," but it was impossible to stem the terrible assault, and Fort Parker fell. Then began the carnival of death. Elder John Parker, Silas M. Parker, Ben F. Parker, Sam M. Frost and Robert Frost were killed and scalped in the presence of their horror-stricken families. Mrs. John Parker, Granny Parker and Mrs. Duty were dangerously wounded and left for dead, and the following were carried into a captivity worse than death: Mrs. Rachel Plummer, James Pratt Plummer, her two-year-old son, Mrs. Elizabeth Kellogg, Cynthia Ann Parker, nine years old, and her little brother John, aged six, both children of Silas M. Parker.

The remainder of the party made their escape, and after incredible suffering, being forced even to the dire necessity of eating skunks to save their lives, they reached Fort Houston, now the residence of Hon. John H. Reagan, about three miles from the present City of Palestine, in Anderson County, where they obtained prompt succor, and a relief party buried their dead.

We will now attempt briefly to follow the fortunes of the poor captives. The first night after the massacre the savages camped on an open prairie, near a water-hole, staked their horses, pitched their camp and threw out their videttes. They then brought out their prisoners, stripped them and tied their hands behind them and their feet together with rawhide thongs, so close and tight as to cut their flesh. Then throwing them upon their faces, the braves gathered around them with the yet bloody, dripping scalps of their martyred kindred, and began their usual war-dance, alternately dancing, screaming, yelling, stamping upon their helpless victims and beating their naked bodies with bows and arrows until the flowing blood almost strangled them. These orgies continued at intervals through the terrible night, which seemed to have no end, these frail women suffering and compelled to listen to the cries of their tender little children. Mrs. Kellogg, more fortunate than the others, soon fell into the hands of the Keechi Indians, who, six months later, sold her to the Delawares, who carried her to Nacogdoches, where this writer then lived, a small child with his parents. Here she was ransomed for $150 by General Sam Houston, who promptly restored her to her kindred. Mrs. Rachel Plummer remained a captive for eighteen months, suffering untold agonies and indignities, when she was finally ransomed by a Santa Fe trader named Wm. Donahue, who soon after escorted her to Independence, Missouri, from whence she finally made her way back to Texas, arriving February 19, 1838. Her son, James Pratt Plummer, after remaining a prisoner six years, was ransomed at Fort Gibson and reached his home in Texas in February, 1843, then aged eight years. During Mrs. Plummer's captivity she again became a mother. When her child was six months old, finding it an impediment to the menial labors imposed upon her as a slave, a Comanche warrior forcibly took it from her arms, and tying a lariat around its body and mounting his horse, dragged the infant at full speed around the camp in sight of the agonized mother until life was extinct, when its mangled remains were tossed back into her lap with savage demonstrations of delight.

This leaves of the sorrowing captives only Cynthia Ann Parker and her little brother John, held by separate bands.   John grew up to athletic young manhood, married a beautiful night-eyed young Mexican captive, Donna Juanita Espinosa, escaped from the savages, or was released by them, joined the Confederate army under General H. P. Bee, became noted for his gallantry and daring, and at latest accounts was leading a happy, contented, pastoral life as a ranchero, on the Western Llano Estacado of Texas.

Four long and anxious years had passed since Cynthia Ann was taken from her weeping mother's arms, during which time no tidings had been received by her anxious family, when in 1840 Colonel Len Williams, an old and honored Texan, Mr. Stout, a trader, and Jack Harry, a Delaware Indian guide, packed mules with goods and engaged in an expedition of private traffic with the Indians.   On the Canadian River they fell in with Pahauka's Band of Comanches, with whom they were peaceably conversant.   Cynthia Ann was with this tribe and from the day of her capture had never beheld a white person.   Colonel Williams proposed to redeem her from the old Comanche who held her in bondage, but the fierceness of his countenance warned him of the danger of further mentioning the subject. Pahauka, however, permitted her reluctantly to sit at the root of a tree, and while the presence of the white men was doubtless a happy event to the poor, stricken captive, who in her doleful captivity had endured everything but death, *she refused to speak one word*. As she sat there, musing, perhaps, of distant relatives and friends, and her bereavement at the beginning and progress of her distress, they employed every persuasive art to evoke from her some expression of her feelings. They told her of her relatives and her playmates, and asked what message of love she would send them, but she had been commanded to silence, and with no hope of release was afraid to appear sad or dejected, and by a stoical effort controlled her emotions, lest the terrors of her captivity should be increased. But the anxiety of her mind was betrayed by the quiver of her lips, showing that she was not insensible to the common feelings of humanity.

As the years rolled by Cynthia Ann developed the charms of captivating womanhood, and the heart of more than one dusky warrior was pierced by the Ulyssean darts of her laughing eyes and the ripple of her silvery voice, and laid at her feet the trophies of the chase. Among the number whom her budding charms brought to her shrine was Petanocona, a redoubtable Comanche war chief, in prowess and renown the peer of the famous "Big Foot," who fell in a desperate hand-to-hand combat with the famous Indian fighter, Captain Shapley P. Ross, of Waco, the illustrious father of the still more distinguished son, General Sul Ross, now the Governor of Texas. It is a remarkable and happy coincidence that the son, emulating the father's contagious deeds of valor and prowess, afterwards, in single combat, in the valley of the Pease, forever put to rest the brave and knightly Petanocona.   Cynthia Ann, stranger now to every word of her mother tongue, save only her childhood name, became the bride of the brown warrior, Petanocona, bore him three children, and loved him with a fierce passion and wifely devotion evinced by the fact that fifteen years after her capture a party of hunters, including friends of her family, visited the Comanche encampment on the upper Canadian River, and recognizing Cynthia Ann through the medium of her name, endeavored to induce her to return to her kindred and the abode of civilization.   She shook her head in a sorrowful negative, and, pointing to her little naked barbarians sporting at her feet, and the great, lazy chief sleeping in the shade near by, the locks of a score of fresh scalps dangling at his belt, replied: ''I am happily wedded, I love my husband and my little ones, who are his too, and I cannot forsake them.''

The recapture of Cynthia Ann Parker Petanocona, and the thrilling events which preceded it, can be best told in the graphic language of the hero who accomplished it, and I therefore append his modest letter:

EXECUTIVE OFFICE, AUSTIN, April 18th.

MY DEAR GENERAL—In response to your request I herewith inclose you my recollections, after a lapse of thirty years, of the events to which you refer.

In 1858 Major Earl Van Dorn, with the Second Cavalry, U. S. A., one company of infantry to guard his depot of supplies, and one hundred and thirty-five friendly Indians under my command, made a successful campaign against the Comanches, and by a series of well directed blows inflicted terrible punishment upon them.   On the morning of October 1, 1858, we came in sight of a large Indian village on the waters of

Washita River, near what is now known as Fort Sill, in the Indian Territory. They were not apprehensive of an attack and most of them were still asleep. Major Van Dorn directed me at the head of my Indians to charge down the line of their lodges or tents, cut off their horses and run them back on the hill. This was quickly accomplished. Van Dorn then charged the village, striking it at the upper end, as it stretched along a boggy branch. After placing about thirty-five of my Indians as a guard around the Comanche horses, some four hundred in number, I charged with the balance of my Indian force into the lower end of the village. The morning was very foggy, and after a few minutes of firing the smoke and fog became so dense that objects at but a short distance could be distinguished only with great difficulty. The Comanches fought with great desperation, as all they possessed was in imminent peril. Shortly after the engagement became general I discovered a number of Comanches running down the branch, about one hundred and fifty yards from the village, and concluded they were retreating. About this time I was joined by Lieutenant Van Camp, of the U. S. A., and a regular soldier by the name of Alexander. With those and one Caddo Indian I ran to intercept them, thus becoming separated from the balance of my force. I soon discovered that the fugitives were women and children. Just then, however, another posse of them came along, and as they passed I discovered in their midst a little white girl and made the Caddo Indian seize her as she was passing. She was about eight years of age and became badly frightened and difficult to manage when she found herself detained by us. I then discovered, much to my dismay, that about twenty-five Comanche warriors, under cover of the smoke, had cut off my small party of four from communication with our comrades and were bearing down upon us. They shot Lieutenant Van Camp through the heart, killing him while in the act of firing his double-barreled gun. Alexander was next shot down and his rifle fell out of his hands. I had a Sharp's rifle and attempted to shoot the Indian just as he shot Alexander but the cap snapped. Another warrior, named Mohee, whom I had often seen at my father's camp on the frontier when he was an Indian Agent, then seized Alexander's loaded gun and shot me through the body. I fell upon the side upon which my pistol was borne, and though partially paralyzed by the shot, I was endeavoring to turn myself and get my revolver out when the Comanche nearest me drew out a long bladed butcher knife and started to stab and scalp me. It seemed that my time had certainly come. He made but a few steps, however, when one of his companions cried out something in the Comanche tongue and they all broke away and fled in confusion. Mohee, the Indian who shot me, ran only about twenty steps when he received a load of buckshot, fired from a gun in the hands of Lieutenant John Majors, of the Second Cavalry, U. S. A., who, with a party of soldiers, had opportunely come to my rescue. During this desperate melee the Caddo held on to the little white girl, and doubtless owed his escape to that fact; as the Comanches were afraid if they shot the Caddo they would kill the little girl. This whole scene transpired in a few minutes, and Van Dorn, although badly wounded, had possession of the entire village, and the surviving Comanches had fled to the almost impenetrable brushy hills, leaving their dead and their property behind them, consisting of ninety-five dead Indians, a number of wounded and captives, about four hundred horses, and the spoils of their camp. The Texas troops had five

killed and several wounded, including Major Van Dorn
and myself. My recollection is that Lieutenant Van
Camp was a protege of Hon. Thad. Stevens, of Pennsylvania, and had but recently come from West Point.
He was a gallant and chivalrous officer, and though at
times in deadly peril myself, and entirely bereft of all
hope of escape, I shall never forget the emotions of
horror that seized me when I saw the Indian warrior,
standing not five feet away, send his arrow clear to the
feather into the heart of that noble young officer. No
trace of the parentage or kindred of the little girl captive could ever be found, and I adopted, reared and
educated her, giving her the name of Lizzie Ross, the
former being in honor of Miss Lizzie Tinsley, the young
lady to whom I was then engaged to be married, and
who has been my wife since May, 1861. Lizzie Ross,
the captive girl, grew into a handsome young woman,
and married happily, but died a few years since in Los
Angeles, California. I lay upon the battle field for five
days unable to be moved, when a litter was constructed
and I was carried on the backs of my faithful Caddoes
ninety miles to Fort Radziminski. As soon as able, I
returned to my Alma Mater, Wesleyan University,
Florence, Alabama, where I finished my education,
returning to Texas in 1859. At the period of which I
write I was on vacation.

For some time after the battle of the Washita the
Comanches were less troublesome to the people of the
Texas frontier, but in 1859 and 1860 the condition of
the frontier was again truly deplorable. The loud and
clamorous demands of the settlers induced the State
Government to send out a regiment under Colonel M.
T. Johnson for public defense. The expedition, though
a great expense to the State, failed to accomplish anything. Having just graduated and returned to my

home at Waco, I was commissioned as Captain by Governor Sam Houston, and directed to organize a company of sixty men, with orders to repair to Fort Belknap, in Young County, receive from Colonel Johnson all Government property, as his regiment was disbanded, and offer the frontier such protection as was possible from so small a force. The necessity for vigorous measures soon became so pressing, however, that I determined to attempt to curb the insolence of those implacable hereditary enemies of Texas who were greatly emboldened by the small force left to confront them, and to accomplish this by following them into their fastnesses and carrying the war into their own homes. I was compelled after establishing a post to leave twenty of my men to guard the Government property, and give some show of protection to the frightened settlers, and as I could take but forty of my men I requested Captain N. G. Evans, in command of the U. S. troops at Fort Cooper, to send me a detachment of the Second U. S. Cavalry. We had been intimately connected in the Van Dorn campaign in 1858, during which I was the recipient of much kindness from him while I was suffering from the severe wound received in the battle of the Washita. He promptly sent me a Sergeant and twenty well-mounted men, thus increasing my force to sixty. My force was still further augmented by some seventy volunteer citizens under the brave old frontiersman, Captain Jack Cureton, of Bosque County.

On December 18, 1860, while marching up Pease River I had suspicions that Indians were in the vicinity by reason of the great number of buffalo which came running toward us from the north, and while my command moved in the low ground I visited neighboring high points to make discoveries. On one of these sand hills I found four fresh pony tracks, and being satisfied that Indian videttes had just gone I galloped forward about a mile to a still higher point, and riding to the top, to my inexpressible surprise, found myself within two hundred yards of a large Comanche village, located on a small stream winding around the base of a hill. It was a most happy circumstance that a cold, piercing wind from the north was blowing, bearing with it clouds of dust, and my presence was thus unobserved, and the surprise complete. By signalling my men as I stood concealed they reached me without being discovered by the Indians, who were busy packing up, preparatory to a move. By the time my men reached me the Indians had mounted and moved off north across the level plain. My command, including the detatchment of the Second Cavalry, had outmarched and become separated from the citizen command of seventy, which left me about sixty men. In making disposition for the attack the Sergeant and his twenty men were sent at a gallop behind a chain of sand hills to encompass them and cut off their retreat, while with my forty men I charged. The attack was so sudden that a large number were killed before they could prepare for defense. They fled precipitately, right into the arms of the Sergeant and his twenty men. Here they met with a warm reception, and finding themselves completely encompassed, every one fled his own way and was hotly pursued and hard pressed. The chief, a warrior of great repute, named Petanocona, with an Indian girl about fifteen years of age mounted on his horse behind him, and Cynthia Ann Parker, his squaw, with a girl child about two years old in her arms and mounted on a fleet pony, fled together. Lieutenant Tom Kelliheir and I pursued them, and, after running about a mile, Kelliheir ran up by the side of Cynthia Ann's horse, and supposing her to be a man was in the act of shooting her when she

held up her child and stopped.   I kept on alone at the
top of my horse's speed after the chief, and about half
a mile further when in about twenty yards of him I fired
my pistol, striking the girl—whom I supposed to be a
man, as she rode like one, and only her head was visible
above the buffalo robe with which she was wrapped—
near the heart, killing her instantly.   And the same
ball would have killed both but for the shield of the
chief, which hung down covering his back.   When the
girl fell from the horse, dead, she pulled the chief off
also, but he caught on his feet, and, before steadying
himself, my horse running at full speed was nearly upon
him, when he sped an arrow which struck my horse
and caused him to pitch or "buck," and it was with
the greatest difficulty I could keep my saddle, meantime narrowly escaping several arrows coming in quick
succession from the chief's bow.   Being at such disad-
vantage he undoubtedly would have killed me, but for
a random shot from my pistol while I was clinging with
my left hand to the pommel of my saddle, which broke
his right arm at the elbow, completely disabling him.
My horse then becoming more quiet, I shot the chief
twice through the body; whereupon he deliberately
walked to a small tree near by, the only one in sight,
and leaning against it with one arm around it for support, began to sing a weird, wild song—the death-song
of the savage.   There was a plaintive melody in it
which, under the dramatic circumstances, filled my
heart with sorrow.   At this time my Mexican servant
who had once been a captive with the Comanches and
spoke their language as fluently as his mother tongue,
came up in company with others of my men.   Through
him I summoned the chief to surrender, but he promptly
treated every overture with contempt, and emphasized
his refusal with a savage attempt to thrust me through

with his lance, which he still held in his left hand. I could only look upon him with pity and admiration, for deplorable as was his situation, with no possible chance of escape, his army utterly destroyed, his wife and child captive in his sight, he was undaunted by the fate that awaited him; and as he preferred death to life, I directed the Mexican to end his misery by a charge of buckshot from the gun which he carried, and the brave savage, who had been so long the scourge and terror of the Texas frontier, passed into the land of shadows and rested with his fathers. Taking up his accoutrements, which I subsequently delivered to General Sam Houston, as Governor of Texas and Commander in Chief of her soldiery, to be deposited in the State Archives at Austin, we rode back to the captive woman, whose identity was then unknown, and found Lieutenant Kelliheir, who was guarding her and her child, bitterly reproaching himself for having run his pet horse so hard after an "old squaw." She was very dirty and far from attractive, in her scanty garments as well as her person, but as soon as I looked her in the face, I said: "Why, Tom, this is a white woman; Indians do not have blue eyes." On our way to the captured Indian village where our men were assembling with the spoils of battle and a large cavalcade of Indian ponies which we had captured, I discovered an Indian boy about nine years old, secreted in the tall grass. Expecting to be killed, he began to cry, but I made him mount behind me and carried him along, taking him to my home at Waco, where he became an obedient member of my family. When in after years I tried to induce him to return to his people he refused to go, and died in McLennan County about four years ago.

When camped for the night, Cynthia Ann, our then unknown captive, kept crying, and thinking it was caused by fear of death at our hands, I had the Mexican tell her, in the Comanche language, that we recognized her as one of our own people and would not harm her. She replied that two of her sons in addition to the infant daughter were with her when the fight began, and she was distressed by the fear that they had been killed. It so happened, however, that both escaped, and one of them—Quanah—is now the chief of the Comanche tribe, and the beautiful City of Quanah, now the county seat of Hardeman County, is named in his honor.   The other son died some years ago on the plains.   Through my Mexican interpreter I then asked her to give me the history of her life with the Indians and the circumstances attending her capture by them, which she promptly did in a very intelligent manner, and as the facts detailed by her corresponded with the massacre at Parker's Fort in 1836, I was impressed with the belief that she was Cynthia Ann Parker.   Returning to my post, I sent her and her child to the ladies at Camp Cooper, where she could receive the attention her sex and situation demanded, and at the same time I dispatched a messenger to Colonel Isaac Parker, her uncle, near Weatherford, Parker County, named as his memorial, for he was for many years a distinguished Senator in the Congress of the Republic and in the Legislature of the State after annexation.   When Colonel Parker came to my post I sent the messenger with him to Camp Cooper in the capacity of interpreter, and her identity was soon discovered to Colonel Parker's entire satisfaction.   She had been a captive just twenty-four years and seven months and was in her thirty-fourth year when recovered.

The fruits of this important victory can never be computed in dollars and cents.   The great Comanche Confederacy was forever broken, the blow was decisive, their illustrious chief slept with his fathers and with him were most of his doughty warriors; many captives were taken, four hundred and fifty horses, their camp equipage, accumulated winter supplies, and so forth.

If I could spare time from my official duties and had patience I could furnish you with many thrilling incidents, never published, relating to the early exploits, trials and sufferings of the early pioneers. My father was appointed Indian Agent in 1856; he had an excellent memory and treasured these until in later life I listened by the hour to their recital. I remain, my dear General,   Sincerely your friend,   L. S. ROSS.

But little of this sad episode remains to be told. Cynthia Ann and her infant barbarian were taken to Austin, the capital of the State; the immortal Sam Houston was Governor, the Secession Convention was in session. She was taken to the magnificent State-house where this august body was holding grave discussion as to the policy of withdrawing from the Union. Comprehending not one word of her mother tongue, she concluded it was a council of mighty chiefs, assembled for the trial of her life, and in great alarm tried to make her escape. Her brother, Colonel Dan Parker, who resided near Parker's Bluff, in Anderson County, was a member of the Legislature from that county, and a colleague of this writer, who then represented the Eleventh Senatorial District. Colonel Parker took his unhappy sister to his comfortable home, and essayed by the kind offices of tenderness and affection to restore her to the comforts and enjoyments of civilized life to which she had so long been a stranger. But as thorough an Indian in manner and looks as if she had been native born she sought every opportunity to escape and rejoin her dusky companions, and had to be constantly and closely watched.

The civil strife then being waged between the North and South, between fathers, sons and brothers, necessitated the primitive arts of spinning and weaving, in which she soon became an adept, and gradually her mother tongue came back, and with it occasional incidents of her childhood.   But the ruling passion of her bosom seemed to be the maternal instinct, and she cherished the hope that when the cruel war was over she would at least succeed in reclaiming her two sons who were still with the Comanches.   But the Great Spirit had written otherwise, and Cynthia Ann and Little Prairie Flower were called in 1864 to the Spirit Land and peacefully sleep side by side under the great oak trees on her brother's plantation near Palestine.

Thus ends the sad story of a woman whose stormy life, darkened by an eternal shadow, made her far-famed throughout the borders of the imperial Lone Star State.   When she left it, an unwilling captive, it contained scarce fifty thousand people and was distracted by foreign and domestic war.   To-day it contains three millions and is the abode of refinement, wealth, culture and universal prosperity and happiness.

Cynthia Ann's son has been for some years the popular hereditary chief of the once powerful confederacy of Comanche Indians, which, though greatly decimated by war and the enervating influences of semi-civilization, is still one of the most numerous tribes in the United States.   He is intelligent, wealthy, tall, muscular and graceful in his movements, is the friend of the white man, and rules his tribe with firmness, moderation and wisdom.   They are located on their picturesque Reservation in the Indian Territory, not many miles distant from the City of Quanah, so named in his honor.

A few years since I met the chief in Wichita Falls, and when informed that I had personally known his palefaced mother, Cynthia Ann, or Prelock—as she was called by the Indians—he had a thousand questions to ask about her personal appearance, size, shape, form, height, weight, color of hair and eyes, etc. He gave me a cordial invitation to visit him at his "tepee," or wigwam, near Fort Sill, profusely promising all the fish, game, ponies and *squaws* I desired.''

CHAPTER XXIX.

HOW QUANAH BECAME CHIEF—HIS COURTSHIP OF
YELLOW BEAR'S DAUGHTER—THE LOVERS ELOPE—
THE RENDEZVOUS ON THE CONCHO RIVER—"STEAL-
ING HORSES ALL OVER TEXAS"—PURSUED AND
OVERTAKEN—YELLOW BEAR'S "BLOW OUT" IN
FORT WORTH.

GENERAL ALFORD'S statement that Quanah is
the hereditary chief is incorrect. He is the son
of a chief, it is true; but sons of Indian chiefs do not
succeed to chieftaincies by the "divine right" of inherit-
ance, but by force of courage, character and ability.
Besides, I have Quanah's own account of how he became chief, and the story is far more romantic, as it is
also less tragic, than the painfully thrilling stories of the
capture and recapture of his ill-fated mother. He narrated it to me on two or three different occasions when
I happened to be in camp with him on the prairies, and
I never lost interest in the rehearsal. Although he
speaks English only brokenly, and is modest and retiring in disposition, he is an exceedingly entertaining

conversationalist on topics within the range of his knowledge, his descriptive powers being really extraordinary,
considering the meagerness of his vocabulary.   Much
of the charm is in the simplicity and directness of his
style, and the aptness of his illustrations from nature.

A COMANCHE BOY.

By the death of his father and the recapture of his
mother Quanah was left an orphan at an age which
could not have been more than twelve years.   The
same disaster that reduced him to orphanage, also made
him a pauper.   Although the son of a deceased chief,
now having no parents, no home and no fortune, he
became, not the ruler of his tribe, but a waif of the

camp.   But being self-reliant, an expert archer, a successful hunter for one of his age, good natured and intelligent, he made friends among the boys of the tribe at least, and found whereon to lay his head, and plenty to eat and wear.   And while orphanage and poverty entailed sorrow and suffering upon the young savage, it was happily contrary to nature for those sad misfortunes to divest him of the "divine right" to love and be loved.   And although he was half a savage by blood and a complete one by habit and association, abundant proof that he was not devoid of the finer instincts of humanity is found in the ardent and constant love which he has always borne for his first wife, Weckeah, and the strong and undying affection and sympathy that he has always exhibited for his most unhappy mother.   It is said that his first question upon surrendering the tribe to General Mackenzie, in 1876, was concerning her, and that his first request was for permission to go to see her, her death not then being known either to himself or the General.

Proof of his captive-mother's love for him, and the sentiment of her nature, are shown in the name which she bestowed upon him, its meaning in the Comanche language being *fragrance*.   I was one day on the prairie with a large party of Comanches.   We stopped at a spring for water, and the chiefs Tabananaka and White

Wolf, the Jonathan and David of the tribe, walked down the branch a short distance and gathered a large handful of wild mint. Holding it to my nose, White Wolf said: "Quanah, quanah. You take it." I said: "Sweet smell. Is that quanah?" They replied: "Yes; quanah—heap good smell." Then plucking a bunch of wild flowers they inhaled their fragrance to show me what they meant, and then handing them to me, said: "Quanah—quanah—heap quanah—good smell."

Quanah's best friend and most constant playmate in his orphanage was Weckeah, Chief Yellow Bear's daughter. They rode her father's ponies to the water-holes, played through the camps together, and were inseparable. He shot antelope and other game for her amusement, and she learned to bead his moccasins and ornament his bow-quiver.

The years went by and Quanah and Weckeah were no longer pappooses. They were in the very bloom of young manhood and womanhood, and each in form and feature without flaw or blemish. But they did not know that they loved one another.

There were other young men in the village, however, and one day one of them, gaudily painted and bedecked with beads and small mirrors, came near Yellow Bear's tepee, blowing his reed flutes. Three days later he came again, and nearer than before. Only two days passed until he came the third time. Spreading his blanket on the grass in front of Yellow Bear's tepee, and seating himself on it, he looked straight at the doorway and played softly all the love songs of the tribe. Weckeah showed not her face to the wooer. Her heart was throbbing violently with a sensation that had never thrilled her before, but it was not responsive to the notes of the flutes.

Nor had Quanah been unobservant, and now there were strange and violent pulsations through his veins also. It was the first time he had ever seen the arts of the lover attempted to be employed on Weckeah. Instantly his very soul was aflame with love for her. There was just one hot, ecstatic, overpowering flush of love, and then there came into his leaping heart the chilling, agonizing thought that this wooing might be by Weckeah's favor or encouragement. Then a very tempest of contending emotions raged in his breast.

When the sun's rays began to slant to the east, there came to Yellow Bear's tepee a rich old chief by the name of Eckitoacup, who had been when a young man the rival of Petanocona for the heart and hand of the beautiful "White Comanche," Cynthia Ann Parker. Eckitoacup and Yellow Bear sat down together on buffalo robes under the brush wickiup in front of the tepee.

They smoked their pipes leisurely, and talked a long time, not in whispers, but very slow and in low tones.

QUANAH AND WECKEAH.

When Quanah and Weckeah met that evening it was with feelings never experienced before by either of them.

Weckeah was greatly agitated. She fluttered like a bird, and kneeling at Quanah's feet, she locked her arms around his knees, looked up in his face and begged him to save her.

The lover with the flutes was Tannap, the only son of rich old Eckitoacup. Weckeah abhorred him, but his father had offered Yellow Bear ten ponies for her. Yellow Bear loved his daughter, and notwithstanding it was the tribal custom he was loth to sell her against her will. He had given Eckitoacup no answer for the present, and Weckeah implored Quanah to get ten ponies and take her himself.

Quanah was filled with deepest pity for Weckeah, and alarmed almost to distraction at the prospect of losing her, for he owned but one pony, and Tannap's father owned a hundred. After telling Weckeah to be brave and note everything said and done in her sight and hearing, Quanah tore away from her and gathering all of his young friends together, explained his situation to them. They loved him and hated Tannap, but calamities in war had made them all poor like himself. They separated to meet again in secret with others next morning. During the day nine ponies were tendered to him, which with the one he owned made ten. These Quanah accepted on condition that others should be received in exchange for them whenever he could get them, which he was ambitious and hopeful enough to believe he could some day do.

Driving these ponies with the haste of an anxious lover to Yellow Bear's tepee, Quanah there met old Eckitoacup, who greeted him with a taunting chuckle of exultation and a look of wicked revenge. His spies having informed him of the action of Quanah's friends, he had raised his bid to twenty ponies. This being an exceptionally liberal offer, Yellow Bear had promptly accepted it, and now the jealous and unforgiving old savage was exulting in his triumph over the poor but knightly rival of his arrogant and despised son, and gloating in his revenge upon the valiant and rising son of his own late successful and hated rival.

Entering the tepee Quanah found Weckeah prostrated at her mother's feet in deepest distress. In two sleeps Tannap would bring the twenty ponies and claim his prize. Weckeah was heartbroken and Quanah was desperate. He hurried back for another consultation with his friends, but not to ask for more ponies. It was to submit a new and startling proposition to them —to tell them of a new thought that had come to him —a new resolution that had taken possession of his very soul. Though he himself did not suspect it, the star of a new chief was about to rise above the horizon.

The new scheme promising spoils and adventure as

well as triumph over a hated rival, Quanah's zealous young friends agreed to it with an enthusiasm which they could hardly avoid showing in their faces and actions.

The unhappy lovers stole another brief twilight meeting in the shadows of Yellow Bear's tepee. Weckeah's quick eyes noted with increased admiration and confidence that the past two days had marked a great change in Quanah. He was now no longer a boy. He seemed to have grown taller, was more serious and thoughtful, and spoke with an evident courage and consciousness of strength which gave her great hope and comfort. He told her their only hope was in flight, and, as she knew, according to the inexorable law of the tribe that meant certain death to him and at least the delivery of herself to Tannap, and possibly death to herself also, if they should be overtaken.

Weckeah, instead of being deterred by the hazards of an attempt at elopement, was eager to go, for in that step she could see the possibility of a life of happiness, and escape from a fate which, in her detestation of Tannap, she regarded as even worse than death.

Just at moondown the next night, which from the description given me I suppose was about 11 o'clock, Quanah and one of his friends met Weckeah at the door of her father's tepee and carried her to the edge of the camp, where their horses and twenty-one other young men were waiting.

And now began the most remarkable elopement, and, in some respects at least, the most remarkable ride ever known on the plains, among either whites or Indians.

Quanah took the lead with Weckeah next behind him, and the twenty-one young men following in single file. For seven hours they did not break a lope except to water their ponies in crossing streams. At daylight they stopped to graze their ponies and make a repast on dried buffalo meat. Here Weckeah saw with pride and increasing confidence that many of those twenty-two tall, sinewy young men carried guns, and all of them revolvers, shields, bows, and quivers full of arrows, and were mounted and equipped throughout as a select war party.

Stopping only a few hours, they changed their course, separated, and came together again at a designated place at sunset. There they stopped again until moondown, and then resuming their journey, traveled together all night.

They were now in Texas, and dared not travel any more in daylight. When night came on they changed their course again, separated into couples, and traveled that way several nights, coming together at a place which from the description I think probably was Double Mountain, in Scurry County, Texas. There they stopped several days to recruit their ponies, subsisting themselves on game, which then abounded in that

COMANCHE BUCKS.

region. From that place they traveled in couples from high point to high point until they came to a river which I suppose from the description was one of the main branches of the Concho, and there they established

their rendezvous and, as Quanah expressed it, "went
to stealin' hosses."

It has been said, indeed I believe it has been universally conceded, that the Comanches, before their subjugation, were "the finest horse thieves the world ever
saw." Whether this has been conceded or not, I am
sure no one who knew them then will deny that it was
a well deserved "compliment." And I doubt not that
Quanah and his bridal party, or bridle party, which ever
it may seem most appropriate to call it, contributed gen-
erously to the weaving of that wreath for the tribal brow.

Eckitoacup's band being utterly unable to follow the
trail, the fugitives remained undiscovered in that region
more than a year, and, in Quanah's own candid and
comprehensive language, "just stole hosses all over
Texas." In a few months they had a large herd, including many valuable American horses and mules.

But it was not long until the young men began to
sigh for "the girls they had left behind them," and to
venture back, a few at a time, to see them, and always
with laudations of their chief, and glowing accounts of
the magnitude and "profits" of their "business." They
invariably returned with their sweethearts, and many
other Indians, of both sexes, also. With Quanah's
encouragement their visits became frequent, and at the
end of a year his band numbered several hundred.

But through these visits old Eckitoacup had heard of the fugitive, and was now coming with a large war party to punish him and take Weckeah. Weckeah

COMANCHE GIRLS AND PAPPOOSE.

again became badly frightened. She would get behind Quanah from the direction of Tannap's approach, clasp her arms around him and beg him not to give her up.

But her entreaties were wholly unnecessary. Quanah, of his own accord, was ready to die rather than suffer her to be taken from him.

Eckitoacup found Quanah's band posted for battle. He was astounded at their numbers and became so alarmed for his own safety that he was glad to agree to an offer of compromise, rather than risk the hazard of battle. Four chiefs were sent from each side to meet half way between the two bands and arrange the compromise. After a great deal of smoking and haggling Eckitoacup's men proposed to accept nineteen horses, the pick of Quanah's herd, in full satisfaction of all demands. Quanah promptly approved the agreement with the cheerful and significant observation that he knew a ranch where he could get nineteen others just as good in a few hours.

This gave Quanah the right to return to the tribe, and as the Texans had him pretty well "located" in that rendezvous and were becoming quite "impudent" and inhospitable to him, and as his band was now too large to be longer concealed anywhere in the State, he followed close after Eckitoacup. Continuing in the Territory to receive accessions from the other bands, including Eckitoacup's, he soon became the acknowledged chief of the tribe, and as a war-chief before being overpowered and conquered he had achieved great renown for prowess, enterprise, sagacity and true military genius.

As General Alford says, he has ruled with firmness, moderation and wisdom, and is very popular with both whites and Indians, his sway perhaps never being greater, or even as great, as it is at the present day. He lives in a picturesque valley on the south side of the Wichita Mountains, where he owns a good home, a hundred horses, perhaps a thousand cattle, and has two hundred and fifty acres of land in cultivation, though I doubt if he has ever plowed a furrow himself, *or would do it if he could*. Weckeah presides over his household, happy, contented, proud of her husband, with immunity from burdensome duties, and provided with all the comforts and luxuries befitting her station in life. But there is a great deal of Brigham Young or Sultan of Turkey in this untutored Comanche, and instead of Weckeah being his only wife, she is merely his favorite in a harem of five—his devotion to her, which has always been constant and unquestioned, not precluding him from the polygamous custom of the tribe. It must be said to his credit, however, that Weckeah is still his favorite. This is quite evident to those who see much of them, and on one occasion when something was said of the possibility of the Government arbitrarily divorcing all the Indians from their plural wives, I asked him

(10)

QUANAH IN CIVILIZED DRESS.

which of his he would choose to retain if that were done. Without a moment's hesitation he said Weckeah.

Yellow Bear, Weckeah's father, became an ardent friend and admirer of Quanah, and lived until 1887, when he got what the Texans considered "a mighty good joke" on himself. He and Quanah got to feeling rich and "civilized," put on their "white man clothes," and went down to Fort Worth to have a big "blow out" with a "herd" of cattle barons who were grazing cattle on their Reservation. They put up at the leading "chuckaway tepee" of the town, the Pickwick, and coming in from a round-up of the city with their white friends at a late hour of the night, they dragged themselves wearily up to their room, and *"blowed out" the gas*. When discovered next morning Yellow Bear's spirit had been blown away to the boundless prairies of the Great Spirit above, never to return, and Quanah was crouched on his "all-fours" at a window, unconscious, his own soul just about to wing its flight to the same mysterious realms.

CHAPTER XXX.

FOUR THOUSAND INDIANS—A SOCIAL CALL FROM THE
CHIEFS—AN ECLIPSE OF THE MOON—PANDEMONIUM
—SUPERSTITIONS AND RELIGIOUS THEORIES—BURIAL
CUSTOMS—HUMOROUS ANECDOTES.

ON the night of July 23, 1888, there was a total
eclipse of the moon. All the Indians on the
Reservation were encamped at the Agency, receiving a
payment from cattlemen who have a large portion of
their lands leased for grazing purposes.

Early in the evening I received a social call at my
house from a party of chiefs composed of Quanah, Wild
Horse, Black Horse and Cheevers, Comanches; Lone
Wolf, Cat, Big Tree, Big Bow, Stumbling Bear and
Tohausen, Kiowas; White Man and Tohau, Apaches,
and Tehuacana Jim and Achittawax, Wichitas.

They were accompanied by Mr. Thomas F. Wood-
ard, an exceptionally intelligent and truthful interpreter,
and I had an unusually interesting conversation with
them on general topics, much of it being of a reminiscent

TEHUACANA JIM (Chief of the Wichitas) AND HIS WIVES.

character. It was just at the time of the capture at Auckland, New Zealand, of Maxwell, the Englishman who had murdered his companion, Preller, in St. Louis, and fled to Australia. I told the Indians how a telegraph message, or "wire paper," as they would say, had been sent entirely around the earth to notify the officers at Auckland to intercept him. They manifested some interest in the story, but not the least amazement, either because they were incapable of comprehending the magnitude of the achievement, or because Indians do not regard anything as impossible to a white man.

Wishing to see if I could astonish them I asked them if they knew the shape of the earth. They looked at one another and hesitated to answer. Finally Quanah said in a cautious sort of way that he had been told that it was "sorter round." To that old Black Horse retorted in a tone of very positive incredulity:

"Y-e-s; I've heard that too; but I've ridden over as much of it as any other man, and it's every bit *flat*, just like this part here. Look out over the prairie here and you can see for yourselves that it's flat; and it's just the same all the way to Washington City and Mexico. I've been to both places. That's just a lie that some white man has started to fool somebody, but anybody ought to have more sense than to believe it."

I thought of the good old deacon who was expelled

from church for telling his brethren that he had seen ice in the summer time, and concluded that I would not try any further to astonish Black Horse concerning the shape of the earth.

Believing, however, that I could "paralyze" him on the eclipse, I asked them if they knew that the moon would "go to sleep" that night. They all said no. I told them that in about two hours from that time it would do so. Old Black Horse straightened up and wanted to know how I knew.

"Oh," I replied, "it's no trick at all for white people to tell beforehand when such things are going to happen. You don't know but what they have something to do with bringing them about."

He shook his head and said, "No; there's no accounting for a white man. He's liable to do anything."

The information made them all uneasy, and in a few minutes they asked me if it was really true, and on being assured that it was, they said they would return to camp and announce it to all the Indians, for not one of them knew it was going to happen. Mr. Woodard laughingly remarked that I "would hear pandemonium break loose when it did happen, too."

After their departure everything was unusually still and silent in the camps until the eclipse began to show, and then Mr. Woodard's remark was very soon verified.

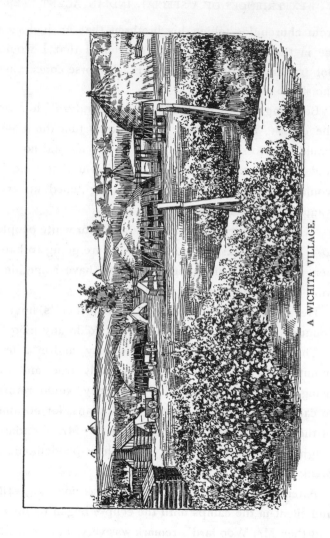

A WICHITA VILLAGE.

At first I could hear the chiefs and medicine men shouting to the Indians as if giving them directions what to do. Then they all commenced to yell and rattle chains and tin pans, and fire off guns and pistols. That set the ponies to running and neighing, and five thousand dogs to barking. As the eclipse grew darker the firing and accompanying noises increased until the din was absolutely deafening.

Before the eclipse became total the noises were abated somewhat, apparently from sheer exhaustion of the Indians. Just at that time I received a dispatch from Philadelphia announcing the death of a chief named Shaddataka, who was in that city with a show. I sent Mr. Woodard to interpret the message to his family. They and his entire band immediately set up a terrible wail of lamentation. Two daughters of the old chief, Wild Horse, who had visited me in the evening, were very sick, and within five minutes of the receipt of the news of Shaddataka's death, one of them expired. Then the camp became a veritable bedlam. The eclipse was not yet total, but it was so nearly so that it was quite dark—a peculiar, weird darkness. Scores of the Indians were still firing guns and pistols. Squaws were still beating tin pans, rattling chains and singing weird songs, the medicine men were yelling, the ponies running and neighing, the dogs barking, and all of the two bereaved bands, both men and women, crying at the top of their voices. The women cut off their hair, daubed mud on their heads, and gashed their faces, arms and breasts with knives in the most horrible manner. Just as the eclipse became total, and when the first outburst of lamentation had begun to subside, Wild Horse's other daughter died. Then the scene became absolutely indescribable, and I believe even beyond the power of imagination. The whole camp was in a terrible frenzy of grief and consternation.

The crying of Indians is entirely different from the sobbing and weeping of white people. Adult Indians of both sexes bawl like children. I have seen old men crying loud enough to be heard half a mile. To hear even one is distressing, and the wail of the entire camp, both men and women, is simply awful.

It was 3 o'clock in the morning before there was any sleep for either whites or Indians. Next morning the Indians all looked haggard and dejected. Noticing that all of their belts were empty of cartridges I asked them if they had any left. They replied: "No more cartridges. Shoot 'em all away. Got none now."

There were near four thousand Indians in the camps. At least one thousand two hundred were men and boys, and each of them had either a pistol or a Winchester rifle, and hundreds of them had both. I calculated that they must have had an average of ten cartridges apiece. Most of the employes put the average at twenty. At ten, the number of shots fired was twelve thousand; at twenty, it was twenty-four thousand.

These noises were made to frighten the Great Bad Spirit and make it turn the moon loose. The Indians have a religious theory or belief that there are two Great Spirits—a good one and a bad one—and that they are constantly struggling with one another for control of the destinies of the Indian. When they see a shadow coming over the moon they think it is being put out, or put to sleep, by the Great Bad Spirit, and they make loud noises for the double purpose of frightening the Bad Spirit away, and arousing and encouraging the Good Spirit.

They have a great many superstitions. One of them is that the Bad Spirit is manifesting his wrath whenever anything is struck by lightning, and if it happens to be a piece of their property they abandon it forever.

Late one evening the Agency office was struck and almost demolished. The news spread rapidly, and scores of Indians came during the next three days to look at it. They all rode entirely around, stopping at each side and end to take a good look, but not one ventured in, or even dismounted from his pony.

About the fourth day an old Indian who lived on the

WICHITA AND CADDO SCHOOL.

Little Washita, twenty miles distant, came all the way to the Agency to tell me that he had heard that I did not intend to throw the office away, and to ask me if his information was correct. I assured him that it was, and showed him that carpenters were then repairing the damage. He said he was glad to hear it, because his house—a small log cabin—was struck during the same storm, and as it had cost him a great deal of money, and the lightning had knocked just a small hole in the roof that could easily be repaired, he hated to throw it away, as had always been their "road," and had concluded to come and see if I really intended to keep the office, as he had heard. If so, he would keep his house. But if I thought there was any danger of the Great Bad Spirit "hitting at us again" if we continued to use the buildings, why we would better just give them up and "sit down" in new places.

Of course I had patience with the old man, and congratulated him on the sensible conclusion he had come to, explained to him as well as I could what lightning was, and sent him back greatly pleased.

Many superstitions are also seen in the burial customs of the Indians. Some of the tribes bury in caves and ravines, some in trees, and some on top of the ground. Generally the bodies are tightly wrapped in blankets and shawls, and those buried on the ground are usually deposited in sitting postures, and walled in with rocks. Those buried in trees are securely fastened and encased on scaffolds tied to the branches. The Poncas and some other tribes bury on scaffolds built six or eight feet high on forked stakes driven in the ground. The air on the plains being extremely dry, it is not unusual to see bodies thus buried pretty thoroughly mummified. Many of the Indian's personal effects are either buried with him or deposited on his grave, and his relatives, instead of planting flowers, bring cooked food for a given number of days and leave it in pans and bowls, for the departed to subsist upon until he completes the journey to the "happy hunting grounds." Sometimes all of his ponies are killed at the grave, but that custom is gradually being broken up by the Agents. Trunks, and things of that sort, however, are frequently seen piled on the graves.

Indians sometimes also make very funny mistakes in trying to adopt the customs of the white people. Some years ago some cattlemen leased a large portion of the Comanche Reservation for grazing purposes. Tabananaka, chief of one of the bands, was opposed to it, but the majority overruled him and he had to submit. He had no confidence in the cattlemen, however, and did not hesitate to charge that they would move their fences and take in more land every time the Indians turned their backs.

To satisfy him on that point somebody suggested that he could get the Agent to swear them. He went to see the Agent and got his promise to do it. When the day came the cattlemen were all on hand with their surveyors, and over a thousand Indians were also present to witness the running of the line, so that if the stakes were ever moved they would know it. But the Agent failed to appear, and the Indians were very much upset.

Finally one of the cattlemen, to avoid delay, inquired of the chiefs why Tabananaka could not swear them himself, just as well as a white chief. Of course the Indians saw no reason why he could not, and after some discussion, it was agreed that he should do it. The stake for the starting point was driven, and all the Indians, fully a thousand of them, stood breathless and on tiptoe to see Tabananaka swear the "wohaw chiefs," as they called the cattlemen. The "wohaw chiefs" removed their hats and held up their right hands and Tabananaka swore them by the Great Spirit above their heads and the mother earth beneath their feet that they would never pull up or destroy that stake or move their fence away from it, and told them very pointedly that if they ever did they would certainly "hear something drop" mighty quick. The cattlemen crowded around him and complimented him extravagantly on the skill and ability which he displayed in the proceeding, but they had failed to notice that the oath only applied to that particular stake.

Two hundred yards up the line the surveyors set another small stake, and all hands were going right on when Tabananaka commanded them to halt. They asked what was the matter. Tabananaka looked surprised and said: "Here's another stake. Swear to it." The cattlemen laughed and said: "Why, you swore us at the other one. Once is enough." That confirmed Tabananaka's suspicions that they would have to be sworn and watched, too, and he replied: "Yes; and you must swear to all of them, or stop the survey." Of course no cattleman who wants Indian grass and knows his business is going to stand back on a little swearing. So they all jumped to their places, jerked their hats off, raised both hands high enough to have satisfied a stage robber, and swore they "would never monkey with that stob no more, nuther," as one of them expressed it.

This line was about seventy-five miles long. A big post was set every mile, and small stakes between. Tabananaka would not listen to the cattlemen at all, but the surveyors finally convinced him that it would be sufficient to swear them at the mile posts. That was the best compromise they could make with him, and notwithstanding it became very monotonous, they had to stand it.   One of them said that Tabananaka kept enlarging on his oath until towards the last it was an oath, a stump speech, and his opinion of the white man in general and of the "Texas wohaw chief" in particular, all in one.

Jack Stillwell, Judge of the Police Court of El Reno, Oklahoma, and Lewis N. Hornbeck, editor of the *Minco Minstrel*, tell the following story on a Cheyenne chief named Big Wolf.   When the Government paid Big Wolf his share of the purchase money of the Cheyenne and Arapahoe Reservation he went to town to buy a hack.   Among the stock of hacks and buggies was a $300 hearse.   The plumes and white metal platings arrested the old man's attention, and when the dealer showed him that he could lay down inside and see out through the glass sides as he traveled along, the bargain was closed.   He paid the $300, hitched in his two little ponies, put his wife up on the box to drive, and then shut himself up inside, to travel with the dignity and style becoming a man of his wealth and station.

The Comanches are very playful Indians.   They are fond of story-telling, and enjoy a joke as well as a white man, as, in fact, most Indians do.   On one occasion I spent several days on the prairies with about six hun-

KIOWA AND COMANCHE SCHOOL.

dred of that tribe and a few Kiowas and Apaches. Having a good interpreter and plenty of smoking tobacco and cigarette paper with me, it was no trouble to get the chiefs around my camp fire every evening.

Seeing that I enjoyed their reminiscences and jokes on one another, they told old Black Horse that he must tell me about his capture of the "black white man." The old fellow had never taken any part in our conversations, and I was desirous of hearing him relate an anecdote, because next to Quanah he had perhaps had the most eventful career of any Indian on the Reservation. For many years he was a terror to the frontier settlements of Texas, but he now has the respect and confidence of every white man who knows him, and is really one of the very best Indians on the Reservation. He is an ugly old fellow, however, of very slight form, lame from numerous wounds received on the warpath, very dark, and battered and scarred almost out of shape.

He demurred at first, but finally related the story as follows:

"A long time ago—maybe so thirty snows, maybe so forty, I dunno—I went with a large war party on a raid into Mexico. We went far enough south to see hundreds of monkeys and parrots. We thought the monkeys were a kind of people, and captured two of them one day. That night we whipped them nearly to

death trying to make them talk, but they would not
say a word, just cry, and finally we turned them loose,
more puzzled than ever to know what they were.''

"On the return trip we came back through Texas.
One day I was scouting off to one side alone, and met
a man riding through the mezquite timber.   He started
to run and my first thought was to kill him, but just as
I was about to send an arrow he looked back over his
shoulder and I saw that his skin was as black as a crow
and that he had great big white eyes.   I had never
seen or heard of that kind of a man, and seeing that he
was unarmed I determined to catch him and take him
to camp alive, so that all the Indians could see him.   I
galloped around in front of him with my bow and arrow
drawn, and he was heap scared.   He fell off of his mule
pony and sit down on his knees and hold his hands up
high and heap cry and say:

"Please, Massa Injun, don't kill poor nigger! *Please*,
Massa Injun, don't kill poor nigger! Bi-yi-yi! *Please*,
Massa Injun, don't kill poor nigger!   Bi-yi-yi!''

Although at that time Black Horse did not know a
word of English and can speak but few even now, the
negro's crying and begging made such an impression
on him that, with his common Indian gift of mimicry,
he can imitate it in a wonderfully natural manner to
this day.   Continuing, he said: ''The black white man

was heap poor. His pony was an old mule that could not run fast at all. His saddle was 'broke' all over, and his bridle was made of ropes. His clothes were dirty and all 'broke' full of holes, and his shoes were all gone—got none at all.''

"I started back with him, and on the way we came to a deep water hole. I was nearly dead for a drink, and motioned to the 'black white man' to get down and drink too. He got down but shook his head to say that he did not want to drink. He was heap scared —just all time shake, and teeth rattle, and all time cry, and maybe so pray to Great Spirit to make Indian turn him loose, and he be a good man and never make it (the Great Spirit) mad any more, and heap o' things like that. I lay down to drink. The bank was sloping and my feet were considerably higher than my head. Suddenly, the 'black white man' caught my back hair with one hand and my belt with the other and raised me away up over his head with my face upward. Before I could do a thing he pitched me headforemost away out in the middle of the water hole. I went clear to the bottom, and when I came to the top and rubbed the water out of my eyes, I saw the 'black white man' running off on my pony, kicking with both feet and whipping with his hat. I rode his old 'mule pony' back to camp and all the Indians heap laugh at Black Horse.''

CHAPTER XXXI.

ORDERED TO WASHINGTON—DETAINED THERE TWO
MONTHS—RETURN TO THE AGENCY—THE INDIANS
STARVING—CHIEF CAT'S PROPOSED "LETTER" TO
WASHINGTON—RELIEVED AT ANADARKO—TO VARI-
OUS AGENCIES—IN CHARGE OF THE INDIAN SCHOOL
AT GENOA, NEBRASKA, AS ACTING SUPERINTENDENT
— APPOINTED INSPECTOR — TERMINATION OF MY
"EXPERIENCES" AS SPECIAL AGENT.

ON the first of December I was ordered to Washington to represent the Indian Office in an appeal
which the deposed Agent at Anadarko had made for
reinstatement. The Secretary of the Interior and the
President taking their own time in the case, I was detained there two months, and had about seven weeks of
uninterrupted sightseeing.

I visited the Capitol occasionally and was sometimes
greatly interested in the proceedings of Congress. The
Supreme Court was also a great attraction for me, and
I rarely ever passed the door of the chamber without
going in to take a look at the learned old gentlemen in

black gowns, and hear them expound the law from the bench. To me there was always a charm in their oral delivery of the opinions not found in the print—their manner being so dignified and decorous, and yet so simple and unaffected; their faces beaming with the light of intelligence, honesty and virtue, and their decisions so clear and so replete with plain and unbe-clouded justice. I was present when Mr. Justice Lamar took his seat, and also when Chief Justice Waite handed down his last opinion.

I spent considerable time strolling through the various great department buildings of the Government —the Patent Office, the Treasury Building, the Post Office Department, and the magnificent new building of the War, State and Navy Departments. Corcoran's Art Gallery, the Smithsonian Institution, the National Museum, and the Washington Navy Yard also pos-sessed many attractions for me. I also made visits to Arlington and Mount Vernon. Arlington is the old home of Robert E. Lee, and is situated on a bluff on the Virginia side of the Potomac River, in sight of Washington. It now belongs to the Government, having been confiscated and converted into a national cemetery during the war. After the war the Supreme Court held the confiscation to have been unlawful, and awarded the Lee heirs certain compensation for the property.   The old mansion is carefully preserved in its original condition and appearance, and all visitors are treated with courtesy.   Mount Vernon is situated on a bluff overlooking the Potomac, seventeen miles below Washington, and is said to look to-day almost exactly as it did in Washington's lifetime.   It is now owned and preserved to the public by the Ladies' Mount Vernon Association, and is the mecca of all patriotic visitors to the national capital.

During my absence the Agency beef and flour contractors had both failed, and when I got back to Anadarko on the first of February many of the Indians were actually starving.   The employes had been keeping them pacified several days with assurances of my early return.   A delegation of Kiowa chiefs met me at the office and seemed greatly disappointed at my failure to bring the beef and flour with me.   But not having heard a word from either of the contractors, of course I could not even give the famishing Indians any satisfactory information, and they returned to camp to meet the whole tribe in council and decide what to do.   In that council it was agreed that it was useless to write a letter to Washington.   They would have to get a white man to write it for them, and he might say what they told him to or he might not—they would never know.   And whether he did or not it would not move Washing-

LONE WOLF. (Chief of the Kiowas.)

ton. They had tried that plan before, and always without success. The only way to attract the notice of Washington was to kill somebody. Whenever they did that he would stop to listen, and send somebody quick to see what was the matter. It would be time lost to write a letter. They must kill somebody, and be quick about it, too, for their women and children were crying for something to eat. But who should be the victim? Cat, a good friend of mine, argued that question in substance as follows:

"Here are Tom Woodard, Bill Shirley, Fred Schlegel, Jim Carson, Joe Becker, George Madera, Jack Nestell, Major Campbell, George Rose and Dr. Graves—all been here long time. Maybe so Washington forgot all about them—all same as forgot about Injun. Injun kill one of them, maybe so Washington never hear about that. Injun kill all of 'em, maybe so Washington not much care—no ask it what's the matter. Heap o' trouble, too, to kill lots o' white men like that. White man heap big fool. Maybe so git mad and heap shoot and kill it some Injuns. Cat no like it, that. But Washington see Agent, just little bit ago. Maybe so Washington no forget about Agent. Injun kill Agent, maybe so Washington hear about that purty quick and send it a wire paper and say, 'what's the matter now? Injun hungry? All right. I send it something to eat purty quick.' That's the best way. Kill Agent. That not much hard work, and Washington come quick to ask it what's the matter.''

Cat's argument prevailed, and it was agreed that he and Komalta, Polant and Little Robe should come to the office early next morning and ask me every two or three hours through the day if I had heard anything from the beef and flour. If I did not give them some definite and satisfactory information by the middle of the afternoon they were then to stab me to death with knives. Agreeably to this programme they appeared at the Agency about 8 o'clock. Taking no notice of several chairs in the office, they seated themselves on the floor around the stove, made a lot of cigarettes, took a comfortable smoke, and then without the least manifestation of unusual concern asked me if I had heard anything of the beef and flour. The negative answer which they received produced no more perceptible effect on them than it would have done on wooden men. But about 9 o'clock, and while they were still lolling about the office, an Indian arrived in a lope with the news that the contractor's men had camped with a herd of beef cattle twelve miles down the river the night before, and would be in sight of the Agency in two hours. This news produced a perfect jubilee. Cat shook hands with me with many demonstrations of joy and affection, entirely unsuspecting that some of the Kiowas who opposed that method of attracting Washington's attention, perhaps through fear of the conse-

MY DEAR OLD FRIEND, CAT.

quences, and a disposition to court favor with the Agent, had come direct from the council and made a full disclosure to me.

Notwithstanding I was to be the victim, I could not find it in my heart to condemn Cat for his contemplated action in this case. Polant and Komalta were two of the most turbulent Indians on the Reservation, and I never believed that Little Robe was very much better; but Cat was really a good Indian, and I am sure he thought a great deal of me and was only going so sacrifice me that his famishing women and children might live. In their situation, and with their experiences in previous emergencies, they believed that was the only "letter" they could "write" to Washington that would bring prompt and adequate relief to their starving families. That being true, would not their action have been sanctioned by the first law of the white man—that of self-preservation? I thought so, and within myself I did not believe any white people on earth would have borne their neglect half as long or half as patiently as they did.

In September Major W. D. Myers, of Pleasant Hill, Missouri, was appointed Agent, and on the first of October, eight months after my return from Washington, he arrived at Anadarko and relieved me of the Agency.

My term of service there as Acting Agent had been eleven months, and during that time I had become warmly attached to many of the Indians and white persons resident on the Reservation—employes, missionaries, traders, and citizens by marriage with Indians.

DR. W. W. GRAVES.

Of the Agency and school employes Dr. W. W. Graves, physician; J. K. P Campbell, clerk; G. A. Hale and W. B. White, storekeepers; J. W. Carson, general foreman and chief of police; Webb Hendrix and George D. Madera, farmers; Lyon Bingham, W. C. Graves and Ed Parish, herders; Thomas F. Woodard, miller and general utility man; Fred Schlegel, blacksmith; J. A. Becker, carpenter, Wm. Shirley, interpreter, and N. Z. Hurd, issue clerk at Fort Sill: Lewis N. Hornbeck, superintendent; Miss Mollie A. Higgins, matron; Mrs. Letitia Hornbeck and Miss Katie B. Hoshall, teachers of the Kiowa school: J. W. Haddon, superintendent; Miss Belle Fletcher and Miss Hattie V. Weir, matrons; Mrs. Fannie C. White and Miss Louise Wallace, teachers of the Wichita school, and George W. Rose, school carpenter, were always obedient and faithful, and generally efficient, in the performance of their duties. And as members of the Indian police force who never disobeyed an order or shirked a duty I still remember Captain Arco, Lieutenant Kohta, and privates Kopeta, Yellow Fish, Wauknakodoke, Kokoon, Satanta, Achittawax and Chaddlekaungky.

From Anadarko I proceeded by way of Darlington and Oklahoma Station to Ardmore, in the Chickasaw Nation, where I had to investigate a dispute over a coal mine. Five different companies had been incorporated under the Chickasaw laws, and each had laid out an extensive claim covering the mine in question. I reported in favor of the Bodine Coal Company, whose officers were J. B. Bodine and Samuel Zuckerman. Upon completing that duty I returned to the Cheyenne and Arapahoe Agency, where I was occupied several days investigating charges of misconduct against the Agent and one of the traders. From Cheyenne and Arapahoe I proceeded to Ponca, Pawnee, Otoe and Oakland, to make another general inspection of that Agency. Agent Osborne had been having considerable trouble at Otoe, but since my last visit he had secured a new clerk for that place—Mr. J. P. Woolsey—with whom he was greatly pleased, and who was handling all of the affairs of that troublesome little Sub-Agency with marked success. My next stop was at Muscogee, where I sojourned a week with Colonel Owen, of the Union Agency, and Colonel D. M. Wisdom, his very excellent chief clerk. From Muscogee I continued on by way of Vinita to the Quapaw Agency. About a week after my arrival at that place I received an order by telegraph to proceed immediately to Genoa, Nebraska. I departed on the next train by way of Springfield, Missouri, Kansas City and Omaha. In the latter city I bought a morning paper, and almost the first item to attract my eye was an announcement from Washington of my appointment by the President to be an Indian Inspector. I was not aware of any vacancy in the Inspectorships at the time, and the news was a great surprise to me.

Genoa is a small town on the Union Pacific Railroad a hundred and thirty miles up the Platte River from Omaha. A large Indian school, known as Grant Institute, is located there. The Superintendent had been removed, and upon my arrival there I found written orders assigning me as Special Agent to the charge of the school as Acting Superintendent. That was the 25th of January, and I remained there in charge of the school until the 12th of March, when I qualified and entered upon duty as an Inspector, and thereby terminated my "experiences" as a Special Agent.

APPENDIX.

ACCORDING to the reports of the Commissioner of
Indian Affairs, the total Indian population of
the United States, exclusive of Alaska, is 247,761.
The names of the Agencies in the various States and
Territories, and the number of Indians at each; the
salaries of the Agents, the number and pay of the
Agency and school employes, and the rules govern-
ing appointments and the granting of traderships, are
as follows:

ARIZONA.

Colorado River Agency.—Indians, 2,527; Agent,
$1,500; clerk and physician, each, $1,000; 5 other
Agency employes, farmer, carpenter, blacksmith, issue
clerk, herder, etc., $360 to $800; superintendent of
school, $1,000; 7 other school employes, teachers,
matron, seamstress, cook, laundress, etc., $150 to $720.

Pima Agency.—Indians, 1,050; Agent, $1,800;

clerk and physician, each, $1,200; 9 employes, $120 to $800; superintendent of school, $1,200; 8 school employes, $480 to $840.

San Carlos Agency.—Indians, 4,977; Agent, $2,000; clerk, physician, engineer and sawyer, each, $1,200; 7 employes, $760 to $900; superintendent of school, $1,200; 15 school employes, $100 to $900; physician Fort Apache Sub-Agency, $1,200; 14 employes, $240 to $540.

Industrial Schools.—At Phœnix: Superintendent, $1,800; clerk, $1,000; farmer, $840.   On Moqui Reservation: Superintendent, $1,500; physician, $1,000; 10 employes, $120 to $840.   At Fort Mojave: Superintendent, $1,500; clerk and physician (one person), $1,000; 12 employes, $120 to $840.

CALIFORNIA.

Hoopa Valley Agency.—Indians, 422; Agent, $1,200; physician, $1,000; 6 Agency employes, $120 to $720; teacher, $72 per month; assistant, $12.

Mission and Tule River Agency.—Indians, 3,779; Agent, $1,600; physician, $1,000; clerk, $900; 2 farmers, $75 per month; superintendent of school, $1,200; 8 teachers, $72 per month; 1, $36.

Round Valley Agency.—Indians, 608; clerk and physician, each, $1,000; 8 Agency employes, $100 to $900; teacher, $80 per month.

Industrial Schools.—At Fort Yuma: Superintendent and physician, each, $1,200; 10 employes, $360 to $720. At Greenville: Teacher, $600. At Perris: Superintendent, $1,500.

COLORADO.

Southern Ute Agency.—Indians, 978; Agent, $1,400; clerk, $1,000; physician, $1,200; 6 employes, $120 to $900.

Industrial School.—At Grand Junction: Superintendent, $1,500; 9 employes, $450 to $900.

IDAHO.

Fort Hall Agency.—Indians, 1,444; Agent, $1,500; clerk, $1,000; physician, $1,200; 14 employes, $16 per month to $840 per year.

Lemhi Agency —Indians, 557; Agent, $1,200; physician, $1,000; 4 employes, $720 to $900; superintendent of school, $800; 5 school employes, $120 to $720.

Nez Perce Agency.—Indians, 1,460; Agent, $1,600; clerk, $1,000; physician, $1,200; 6 employes, $360 to $720; school teacher, 600; industrial teacher, $720; 4 school employes, $480 to $600.

Industrial Schools.—At Fort Hall: Superintendent, $1,500; physician, $1,000; 19 employes, $120 to

$840. At Fort Lapwai: Superintendent, $1,000; 15 employes, $120 to $900.

INDIAN TERRITORY.

Quapaw Agency.—Indians, 1,049; Agent, $1,500; clerk and physician, each, $1,200; 5 employes, $480 to $600; superintendent of school, $1,200; teacher, $1,000; 8 school employes, $48 per month to $600 per year; 22, $180 to $600.

Union Agency.—Indians (five civilized tribes), 61,000; Agent, $1,500; clerk. $1,200; assistant, $900.

IOWA.

Sac and Fox Agency.—Indians, 380; Agent, $1,000; 2 employes, each, $600.

KANSAS.

Pottawatomie and Great Nemaha Agency.—Indians, 1,007; Agent, $1,200; clerk, $1,200; physician, $1,200; 1, $1,000; 14 employes, $300 to $720; 2 superintendents of schools, $720 each; 1, $750; 10 school employes, $300 to $480.

Industrial School.—Haskell Institute, at Lawrence: Superintendent, $2,000; assistant, clerk, physician, and principal teacher, each, $1,200; 55 employes, $120 to $900.

MICHIGAN.

Mackinac Agency.—Indians, 7,313; Agent, $1,800;

clerk and physician, $720 each; superintendent of school, $1,500; 4 teachers, $400 each; 1, $60 per month.

MINNESOTA.

White Earth Agency.—Indians, 6,038; Agent, $1,800; clerk, $1,200; 3 physicians, $1,200 each; superintendent of school, $1,000; 2 $800 each; 1 overseer, $1,000; 42 Agency and school employes, $120 to $900.

MONTANA.

Blackfeet Agency.—Indians, 2,026; Agent, $1,800; clerk and physician, $1,200 each; 18 employes, $120 to $900; superintendent of school, $800; teacher, $720; matron, $480; seamstress and cook, $400 each.

Crow Agency.—Indians, 3,226; Agent, $2,000; clerk and physician, $1,200 each; issue clerk, $1,000; 27 employes, $150 to $900; superintendent of school, $1,000; 10 school employes, $180 to $800.

Flathead Agency.—Indians, 2,280; Agent, $1,500; clerk and physician, $1,200 each; 12 employes, $120 to $900.

Fort Belknap Agency.—Indians, 1,650; Agent, $1,500; clerk and physician, $1,200 each; 18 employes, $120 to 900.

Fort Peck Agency.—Indians, 2,917; Agent, $2,000; clerk and physician, $1,200 each; 14 employes, $120 to $900; superintendent of school, $1,200; 14 school employes, $120 to $900.

Tongue River Agency.—Indians, 795; Agent, $1,500; physician, $1,000; 10 employes, $120 to $900.

NEBRASKA.

Omaha and Winnebago Agency.—Indians, 2,382; Agent, $1,600; clerk, $1,200; physician, $1,000; 9 employes, $180 to $900; superintendent of school, $900; 7 teachers, $500 to $600; 10 other school employes, $420 to $720.

Santee Agency.—Indians, 1,312; Agent, $1,200; physician, $1,200; clerk, $1,000; 19 employes, $150 to $720; school teacher, $60 per month.

Shipping Clerks.—Rushville: Shipping clerk, $1,200; assistant, $600. Valentine: Shipping clerk, $1,200; assistant, $600.

Industrial School.—Grant Institute, Genoa: Superintendent, $2,000; clerk, $1,000; physician, $1,000; 31 teachers, matrons, industrial teachers and other employes, $120 to $900.

NEVADA.

Nevada Agency.—Indians, 4,558; Agent, $1,500; clerk and physician, $1,000 each; 5 employes, $480 to $840; 2 teachers, $72 per month; assistant teacher and matron, $48 per month each.

Western Shoshone Agency.—Indians, 3,680; Agent, $1,500; physician, $1,000; clerk, $900; 19 employes, $360 to $720; superintendent of school, $720.

Industrial School.—At Carson: Superintendent, $1,500; clerk, $1,000; 9 employes, $120 to $900.

NEW MEXICO.

Mescalero Agency.—Indians, 1,202; Agent, $1,600; clerk, $1,000; physician, $1,000; 5 employes, $240 to $720; superintendent of school, $900; 3 employes, $480 to $720.

Navajo Agency.—Indians, 19,277; Agent, $2,000; clerk, $1,000; physician, $1,200; 14 employes, $120 to $900; superintendent of school, $1,000; 10 employes, $120 to $900.

Pueblo Agency.—Indians, 7,762; Agent, $1,500; physician, $1,000; clerk, $1,000; 8 employes, $120 to $900; 3 teachers, $80 per month.

Industrial Schools.—At Albuquerque: Superintendent, $1,000; 35 teachers, clerk, physician, matron, engineer, watchman, tailor, farmers, etc., $48 per month to $600 per year. At Dawes Institute: Superintendent, $1,500; clerk, $1,200; 15 employes, $360 to $960.

NEW YORK.

New York Agency.—Indians, 4,963; Agent, $1,000.

NORTH CAROLINA.

Eastern Cherokee Agency.—Indians, 3,000; Agent, $800; superintendent of school, $1,200.

NORTH DAKOTA.

Devil's Lake Agency.—Indians, 2,182; Agent, $1,200; clerk and physician, $1,000 each; 12 employes, $180 to $900; superintendent of school, $72 per month.

Fort Berthold Agency.—Indians, 1,322; Agent, $1,500; clerk and physician, $1,200 each; 17 employes, $180 to $900.

Standing Rock Agency.—Indians, 4,690; Agent, $1,800; clerk and physician, $1,200 each; issue clerk, $1,000; 57 employes, $120 to $900; superintendent of school, $1,000; 11 teachers, $360 to $840; 12 other school employes, $216 to $480.

Industrial Schools.—At Fort Stevenson: Superintendent, $1,200; 10 employes, $120 to $600. At Fort Totten: Superintendent, $1,800; clerk, $1,000; 15 employes, $240 to $840.

OKLAHOMA.

Sac and Fox Agency.—Indians, 2,261; Agent, $1,200; clerk, $1,000; two physicians, $1,000 each; 5 employes, $300 to $720; superintendent of school, $1,000; 1, $600; 13 school employes, $300 to $700.

Ponca, Pawnee, Otoe and Oakland Agency.—Indians, 1,968; Agent, $1,500. At Ponca: Clerk, $1,200; 8 employes, $480 to $720; superintendent of school, $1,000; 15 school employes, $120 to $720. At Pawnee: Clerk, $1,000; 9 employes, $480 to $720; superintendent of school, $1,200; 9 school employes, $360 to $720. At Otoe: Clerk, $900; physician, $1,200; 4 employes, $300 to $720; superintendent of school, $900; 9 employes, $120 to $600. At Oakland: General mechanic, $720; school teacher, $720.

Osage Agency.—Indians, 1,705; Agent, $1,800; clerk, $1,200; assistant clerk, $1,000; 2 physicians and chief of police, $1,200 each; general mechanic, $1,000; 3 employes, $480 to $600; superintendent of school, $1,000; 3 teachers and one matron, $600 each; 10 other school employes, $300 to $400.

Kaw Sub-Agency.—Indians, 200; superintendent of school, in charge, $900; physician, $1,200; 2 employes, $600 and $720; 9 school employes, $180 to $480.

Kiowa, Comanche and Wichita Agency.—Indians, 4,182; Agent, $2,000; clerk and physician, $1,200 each; 27 employes, $120 to $720; 3 superintendents of schools (2 at Agency and 1 at Fort Sill), $1,000 each; 27 school employes, $150 to $720.

Cheyenne and Arapahoe Agency.—Indians, 3,434;

Agent, $2,200; clerk and physician, $1,200 each; 28 employes, $180 to $900; 2 superintendents of schools, $1,000 each; 2 teachers, $720 each; 6, $600 each; 2 matrons, $600 each; 10 other school employes, $300 to $720.

OREGON.

Grand Ronde Agency.—Indians, 510; Agent, $1,000; physician, $1,000; clerk, $900; 7 employes, $120 to $780; superintendent of school, $900; 1 teacher, $600; 3 school employes, $360 to $480.

Klamath Agency.—Indians, 972; Agent, $1,200; clerk and physician, $1,000 each; 7 employes, $120 to $800; superintendent of school, $1,200; 1, $1,000; 3 teachers, $600 each; 2, $720 each; 10 other school employes, $360 to $600.

Siletz Agency.—Indians, 612; Agent, $1,200; clerk, $900; physician, $1,000; 5 employes, $480 to $800; superintendent of school, $900; 9 school employes, $240 to $720.

Umatilla Agency.—Indians, 894; Agent, $1,200; clerk, $900; physician, $1,000; 4 employes, $300 to $800; superintendent of school, $1,200; 3 teachers, $600 each; 14 other school employes, $400 to $600.

Warm Springs Agency.—Indians, 859; Agent, $1,200; clerk, $800; physician, $900; 4 employes, $500 to $720; superintendent of school, $1,000; 1,

$900; 4 teachers, $600 to $720; 10 other school employes, $120 to $600.

Industrial Schools.—At Chemawa: Clerk and superintendent, $1,200; physician, $1,000; 17 employes, $120 to $900. At Salem: Superintendent, $2,000.

PENNSYLVANIA.

Training School.—At Carlisle: Average attendance of Indian pupils, 560; superintendent, an Army officer; first assistant superintendent, $1,500; assistant superintendent, physician, and principal teacher, $1,200 each; clerk, music teacher, disciplinarian, and matron, $1,000 each; 50 other employes, $120 to $720.

SOUTH DAKOTA.

Cheyenne River Agency.—Indians, 2,965; Agent, $1,500; clerk and physician, $1,200 each; 28 employes, $120 to $900; superintendent of school, $900; 6 school employes, $120 to $600; 5 teachers day schools, $60 per month; 1, $36.

Pine Ridge Agency.—Indians, 4,873; Agent, $1,800; clerk and physician, $1,200 each; 25 employes, $480 to $900; superintendent of school, $1,500; assistant, $1,000; 14 employes, $300 to $720.

Rosebud Agency.—Indians, 8,291; Agent, $2,200; clerk and physician, $1,200 each; 36 employes, $300 to $900; 17 teachers of day schools, $36 to $72 per month.

Yankton Agency.—Indians, 1,776; Agent, $1,600; clerk and physician, $1,200 each; 27 employes, $120 to $900; superintendent of school, $1,200; 18 school employes, $120 to $600.

Sisseton Agency.—Indians, 1,496; Agent, $1,500; clerk and physician, $1,000 each; 6 employes, $180 to $720; superintendent of school, $1,200; 12 school employes, $150 to $720.

Crow Creek and Lower Brule Agency.—Indians, 2,274; Agent, $1,800; 2 clerks and 2 physicians, $1,200 each; 40 employes, $180 to $900; superintendent of school, $1,000; 5 teachers, $240 to $600; 9 other school employes, $120 to $500.

Industrial School.—At Pierre: Superintendent, $1,500; 11 employes, $150 to $900.

UTAH.

Uintah and Ouray Agency.—Indians, 2,598; Agent, $1,800; 2 clerks and 2 physicians, $1,200 each; 17 employes, $240 to $1,000; superintendent of school, $1,200; 2 teachers, $720 to $840; 4 other school employes, $400 to $720.

WASHINGTON.

Colville Agency.—Indians, 3,150; Agent, $1,500; clerk and 3 physicians, $1,200 each; 10 employes, $240 to $900; superintendent of school, $900; 6 school employes, $500 to $720.

Neah Bay Agency.—Indians, 780; Agent, $1,200; clerk and physician, $1,000 each; 9 employes, $120 to $480; teacher day school, $60 per month; 1, $48.

Puyallup and S'kokomish Agency.—Indians, 1,712; Agent, $1,600; clerk, $1,200; 2 physicians, $1,000 each; superintendent of school, $1,200; 2, $900 each; 9 teachers; $600 to $720; 16 school employes, $360 to $500.

Yakama Agency.—Indians, 3,290; Agent, $1,800; clerk and physician, $1,200 each; 12 employes, $500 to $840; superintendent of school, $1,200; 10 school employes, $120 to $720.

Quinaielt Sub-Agency.—Indians, 423; physician in charge, $1,000; 2 employes, $200 to $600; superintendent of school, $900; 11 school employes, $60 to $600.

Tulalip Agency.—Indians, 1,223; Agent, $1,200; physician and clerk, $900; 10 employes, $240 to $720.

WISCONSIN.

Green Bay Agency.—Indians, 3,000; Agent, $2,000; superintendent of logging, $1,800; clerk and physician, $1,200 each; 8 employes, $480 to $900; matron Menomonie hospital, $450; 1 hospital employe, $400; 1, $350; superintendent of school, $1,200; 12 employes, $400 to $720.

La Pointe Agency.—Indians, 3,796; Agent, $2,000; clerk, $1,200; physician, $1,000; 6 employes, $700 to $900; superintendent of schools at Tomah, $1,500; 9 teachers of day schools, $40 to $60 per month.

WYOMING.

Shoshone Agency.—Indians, 1,800; Agent, $1,500; clerk and physician, $1,200 each; engineer, $1,000; 13 employes, $120 to $800; superintendent of Reservation, $1,500; superintendent of school, $1,000; 10 school employes, $180 to $800.

Indians not under an Agent.—In Arizona, 914; in California, 6,456; in Florida, 892; in Idaho, 600; in Maine, 410; in Oregon, 800; in Texas, 290; in Utah, 390; in Wisconsin, 1,210.

Inspectors and Special Agents.—Five Inspectors, $3,000 and actual expenses; five Special Agents, $2,000, all traveling expenses, and $3 per day for personal expenses.

APPOINTMENTS.

Officers and Employes.—The Inspectors and Agents are appointed by the President, and required to give bond. The Civil Service Law now applies to the Agency physicians, and also to the superintendents, assistant superintendents, physicians, teachers and matrons of all the schools, and applications for appointment to those positions should be addressed to "The U. S. Civil Service Commission, Washington, D. C." The Commission should be first written to for blanks and instructions. The Agency clerks, assistant clerks, warehousemen, overseers, farmers, millers, mechanics, blacksmiths, herders, stablemen, teamsters, and laborers; and also all subordinate employes of the Reservation schools, such as assistant matrons, seamstresses, cooks, laundresses, farmers, disciplinarians, and laborers, are now appointed by the Agents, and applications for those places should be addressed, with proper recommendations, to "The U. S. Indian Agent," at the particular Agency where service is desired. The subordinate employes of the industrial and training schools are appointed by the superintendents.

The superintendents of Reservation schools are under the control and supervision of the Agents. But the superintendents of the industrial and training schools are under the direct supervision and control of the Indian Department at Washington—not subject to any Agent—and are required to give bond.

INDIAN TRADERS.

Merchants are licensed by the Indian Office at Washington to trade with the Indians at the various Agencies. Applications have to be made direct to the

Commissioner of Indian Affairs, accompanied by proper recommendations as to moral character, integrity, etc. The licenses have to be renewed annually, but no fee is charged, the applicant only being required to give bond in the sum of $10,000 (on blanks furnished by the Department), conditioned that he will observe the laws governing trade with Indians. The number of traders at each Agency is limited in proportion to the number and income of the Indians, and many of the traderships are very valuable. It is a great advantage to any applicant, either for appointment or for license to trade, to have the assistance at Washington of a Senator or Member of Congress, though many applicants succeed without the help of either.

THE END.

THE WESTERN FRONTIER LIBRARY

of which *Experiences of a Special Indian Agent* is Number
29, was started in 1953 by the University of Oklahoma
Press. It is designed to introduce today's readers to the
exciting events of our frontier past and to some of the
memorable writings about them. The following list is
complete as of the date of publication of this volume:

1. Prof. Thomas J. Dimsdale. *The Vigilantes of Montana*. With an introduction by E. DeGolyer.
2. A. S. Mercer. *The Banditti of the Plains*. With a foreword by William H. Kittrell.
3. Pat F. Garrett. *The Authentic Life of Billy, the Kid*. With an introduction by Jeff C. Dykes.
4. Yellow Bird (John Rollin Ridge). *The Life and Adventures of Joaquín Murieta*. With an introduction by Joseph Henry Jackson.
5. Lewis H. Garrard. *Wah-to-yah and the Taos Trail*. With an introduction by A. B. Guthrie, Jr.
6. Charles L. Martin. *A Sketch of Sam Bass, the Bandit*. With an introduction by Ramon F. Adams.
7. Washington Irving. *A Tour on the Prairies*. With an introduction by John Francis McDermott.
8. *X. Beidler: Vigilante*. Edited by Helen Fitzgerald Sanders in collaboration with William H. Bertsche, Jr. With a foreword by A. B. Guthrie, Jr.

9. Nelson Lee. *Three Years Among the Comanches*. With an introduction by Walter Prescott Webb.

10. *The Great Diamond Hoax and Other Stirring Incidents in the Life of Asbury Harpending*. With a foreword by Glen Dawson.

11. *Hands up; or, Twenty Years of Detective Life in the Mountains and on the Plains:* Reminiscences by General D. J. Cook, Superintendent of the Rocky Mountain Detective Association. With an introduction by Everett L. DeGolyer, Jr.

12. Will Hale. *Twenty-Four Years a Cowboy and Ranchman in Southern Texas and Old Mexico*. With an introduction by A. M. Gibson.

13. Gen. James S. Brisbin, U.S.A. *The Beef Bonanza; or, How to Get Rich on the Plains*. With a foreword by Gilbert C. Fite.

14. Isabella L. Bird. *A Lady's Life in the Rocky Mountains*. With an introduction by Daniel J. Boorstin.

15. W. T. Hamilton. *My Sixty Years on the Plains*. With an introduction by Donald J. Berthrong.

16. *The Life of John Wesley Hardin, As Written by Himself*. With an introduction by Robert G. McCubbin.

17. Elizabeth Bacon Custer. *"Boots and Saddles"; or,*

Experiences of a Special Indian Agent, in its reprinted form, has been designed to approximate the original edition—even to the anomalous placement of the book title on recto running heads.

UNIVERSITY OF OKLAHOMA PRESS
NORMAN